Transforming
CLASSROOM
GRADING

ROBERT J. MARZANO

ASCD

ASSOCIATION FOR SUPERVISION AND CURRICULUM DEVELOPMENT
ALEXANDRIA, VIRGINIA   USA

Association for Supervision and Curriculum Development
1703 N. Beauregard St. • Alexandria, VA 22311-1714 USA
Telephone: 1-800-933-2723 or 703-578-9600 • Fax: 703-575-5400
Web site: http://www.ascd.org • E-mail: member@ascd.org

Gene R. Carter, *Executive Director*
Michelle Terry, *Deputy Executive Director, Program Development*
Nancy Modrak, *Director, Publishing*
John O'Neil, *Director of Acquisitions*
Julie Houtz, *Managing Editor of Books*
Jo Ann Irick Jones, *Senior Associate Editor*
Ernesto Yermoli, *Project Assistant*
Gary Bloom, *Director, Design and Production Services*
Georgia McDonald, *Senior Designer*
Tracey A. Smith, *Production Manager*
Dina Murray Seamon, *Production Coordinator*
Vivian L. Coss, *Production Coordinator*
Barton Matheson Willse & Worthington, *Desktop Publisher*
Coughlin Indexing Services, Inc., *Indexer*

Printed in the United States of America.

September 2000 member book (pcr). ASCD Premium, Comprehensive, and Regular members periodically receive ASCD books as part of their membership benefits. No. FY01-01.

ASCD Product No. 100053
ASCD member price: $18.95   nonmember price: $22.95

Library of Congress Cataloging-in-Publication Data

Marzano, Robert J.
    Transforming classroom grading / Robert J. Marzano.
        p. cm.
Includes bibliographical references (p.) and index.
    ISBN 0-87120-383-9 (alk. paper)
    1. Grading and marking (Students)—United States.   2. School reports—United States.   I. Title.
    LB3060.37 .M27 2000
    371.27'2—dc21
                                          00-009790

04 03 02 01 00   10 9 8 7 6 5 4 3 2 1

To my family:
Jana, Todd, Christine, Carmen, Ashley

Transforming Classroom Grading

List of Figures

The Mandate to Change Classroom Grading

For at least a hundred years, teachers at almost every level have been using grades of some type—letter grades, percentage scores—as the overall indicator of student achievement. Students, parents, and community members also have assumed that these omnibus grades are reliable measures of student achievement. For example, most Americans would interpret a grade of C in a mathematics class as a statement that the student "didn't demonstrate exceptional achievement in the content addressed in the course, but acquired most of what was important." Similarly, a grade of A in a science class would be interpreted to mean that the student "thoroughly understands the content presented in the course." In short, Americans have a basic trust in the message that grades convey—so much so that grades have gone without challenge and are, in fact, highly resistant to any challenge. As education reporter Lynn Olson notes, the use of grades "is one of the most sacred traditions in American education. . . . The truth is that grades have acquired an almost cult-like importance in American schools. They are the primary shorthand tool for communicating to parents how children are faring" (Olson, 1995, p. 24).

Why, then, would anyone want to change current grading practices, given their wide acceptance? Why would anyone write a book that deals with "transforming" grading policies? The answer is quite simple: grades are so imprecise that they are almost meaningless. This straightforward but depressing fact is usually painfully obvious when one examines the research and practice regarding grades with a critical eye.

One basic purpose of this book is to provide educators with a thorough grounding in grading research and theory. To obtain such a perspective requires a discussion of grading at a level of detail not commonly required in most teacher preparation courses or in most books on classroom assessment and grading. Consequently, reading this text may require a level of effort not required when reading other books on the same topic. It is my firm conviction, however, that the end product is well worth the effort. An understanding of the research and theory on current grading will open up new and exciting alternatives in a variety of areas.

Because suggesting a shift in an existing paradigm without offering an alternative can be a dangerous endeavor, a second purpose of this text is to present viable alternatives to current grading policies. This book, then, is clearly intended to create change.

Resistance to Change

It is safe to say that human beings usually resist changing the familiar—particularly characteristics that define an institution. Researchers Tyack and Tobin (1994) explain that the public perceives certain defining characteristics of school as those things that they have come to think of as "real school." Any attempt to alter "real school," according to Tyack and Tobin, is very difficult even when the alteration will clearly produce better results.

Without a doubt, changing the way students are graded alters what people associate with "real school." Consequently, one can expect some opposition to new grading techniques. To illustrate, Olson relates one district's attempt to change the way it graded students and reported student progress on report cards. Parents, administrators, and volunteer community members in the district worked for two years to develop a new report card that represented what they considered "best practice" about grading. To the surprise of those on the report card committee, the new system faced strong negative reactions even after undergoing extensive study and testing. Olson (1995) describes the reaction from the community:

> The three women seated around Dona LeBouef's butcher-block kitchen table look more like a bevy of PTA moms than a rebel army. Dressed in coordinated shirts and pants and denim jumpers, they're articulate and polite. Classical music plays softly in the background as they sip their coffee and review the weapons in their campaign: a large sheaf of photocopied newspaper articles and editorials, old report cards, and petitions.
>
> Their targets are pilot report cards introduced by the public school system here last fall that eliminated traditional letter grades in the elementary schools. The new format, tested citywide, was designed to more accurately reflect the teaching going on in the classroom and to provide families with more detailed information about their children. School officials thought parents would be pleased. They were wrong. (p. 23)

Why were parents upset that the district was trying to make a change that had been studied and was clearly superior to the old approach? Quite simply, the new system required a change in "real school" as perceived by the parents in Dona LeBouef's kitchen.

Although parents in your community will not necessarily oppose changes to local district or school grading and reporting practices, they might. The public trust in education, while strong in some areas, is not unquestioned. Indeed, when a representative sample of U.S. parents were polled about their opinions of teachers and administrators, one of the basic findings was that "educators need to rebuild public trust in a few important areas" (Farkas et al., 1994, p. 36). One of those important areas was the ability to make judgments about individual students.

If a district or school wishes to make changes in current grading and reporting practices, then it is well advised to provide a strong logic for the new system along with a thorough accounting of the inadequacies of the old system. The proposed changes must be communicated to all interested parties: educators and noneducators alike. Additionally, the proposed changes should be well thought out and well tested before they are implemented on a wide scale.

What's Wrong with the Current System?

Educational researchers and theorists have been highly critical of traditional grading practices for quite some time. Researchers Lawrence Cross and Robert Frary explain that "school marks and grading have been the source of continuous controversy since the turn of the century" (1999, p. 53). For example, as far back as 1913, researcher I. E. Finkelstein expressed strong concern about the validity of grading practices:

> When we consider the practically universal use in all educational institutions of a system of marks, whether numbers or letters, to indicate scholastic attainment of the pupils or students in these institutions, and when we remember how very great stress is laid by teachers and pupils alike upon these marks as real measures or indicators of attainment, we can but be astonished at the blind faith that has been felt in the reliability of the marking system. School administrators have been using with confidence an absolutely uncalibrated instrument. . . . What faults appear in the marking systems that we are now using, and how can these be avoided or minimized? (In Durm, 1993, p. 294)

Commenting on Finkelstein's assertion, educational historian Mark Durm notes: "Can we better answer these questions today? Is our grading system still uncalibrated" (1993, p. 294)? Most recently, researcher Tom Guskey (1996b) has also commented on the long history of problems surrounding grading practices. Guskey cites the comments Warner Middleton made in 1933 when Middleton and his col-

leagues were charged with altering their school grading policies:

> The Committee On Grading was called upon to study grading procedures. At first, the task of investigating the literature seemed to be a rather hopeless one. What a mass and a mess it all was! Could order be brought out of such chaos? Could points of agreement among American educators concerning the perplexing grading problem actually be discovered? It was with considerable misgiving and trepidation that the work was finally begun. (In Guskey, 1996b, p. 13)

Like Durm, Guskey laments that the difficulties surrounding grading have not significantly changed in decades: " . . . coming up with prescriptions for best practice seems as challenging today as it was for Middleton and his colleagues more than 60 years ago" (pp. 13–14).

While there is no consensus about the new grading system (Cross and Frary, 1999), there is quite a bit of agreement about what is wrong with the current system. Virtually all of the criticisms focus on one or more of three problem areas: (1) teachers consider many factors other than academic achievement when they assign grades, (2) teachers weight assessments differently, and (3) teachers misinterpret single scores on classroom assessments. Let's briefly consider each of these areas.

Teachers Consider Factors Other Than Academic Achievement

To illustrate the first problem, consider Figure 1.1, which reports the results of a 1996 study at the Mid-continent Regional Educational Laboratory (McREL) in Aurora, Colorado. In this study, 640 teachers of grades K–12 were asked to identify those

FIGURE 1.1
Percentage of Teachers Reporting Use of
Effort, Behavior, Cooperation, and Attendance in Determining Grades

Grade Level	Effort	Behavior	Cooperation	Attendance
K (n = 79)	31%	7%	4%	8%
1–3 (n = 110)	29%	8%	4%	8%
4–6 (n = 158)	30%	8%	8%	10%
7–9 (n = 142)	36%	10%	8%	18%
10–12 (n = 151)	36%	14%	9%	24%

Source: Marzano (1995b). Copyright © 1995 by McREL Institute. Reprinted by permission.

skills and abilities *in addition to* subject-matter content that they consider when assigning grades to students. Figure 1.1 demonstrates the relative importance of the role these "nonachievement" factors can play in grades. For example, consider the responses of the teachers in grades 7–9: 36 percent counted effort in their grading policies; by inference, we know that 64 percent of those same teachers did not. Similarly, 10 percent of the teachers in grades 7–9 counted behavior and 90 percent did not, and so on.

To understand the importance of these findings, assume that two students took exactly the same course from two different teachers. Also assume that exactly the same homework, quizzes, and tests were administered in those courses, and that the two students had identical performance on all of the homework, quizzes, and tests. Finally, assume that they exhibited exactly the same cooperation, effort, and so on in the two classes. Given the similarities in their performance and behavior, one might assume that the two students would receive exactly the same course grade, whether it

was an overall letter grade or an overall percentage. However, the findings in Figure 1.1 indicate that they would not necessarily receive exactly the same grade if the two teachers considered different nonachievement factors. For example, one teacher might include effort, behavior, and cooperation, and the other teacher effort only or none of the nonachievement factors in Figure 1.1. The teacher who counted effort, behavior, and cooperation would probably assign her student a different grade than the one who counted effort only.

Teachers Weight Assessments Differently

The situation just described (including different nonachievement factors) is compounded when one takes into account the second major problem area of current grading practices: differential weighting of assessments. Figure 1.2 illustrates this problem.

This figure depicts the findings of another study conducted at McREL. We asked two teachers who were team teaching a

FIGURE 1.2
Grades Assigned by Two Teachers to Same Students

Student	Grade from Teacher #1	Grade from Teacher #2
Zack	A	B
Jose	A	A
Brian	B	B
Zed	A	A
Terrel	A	A
Lynne	B	C
Natalie	B	B
Nadine	A	D
Ashley	A	B
Sasha	A	C
Devon	A	A
Sarah	A	B
Rosa	A	A
Jung	A	A
Jason	B	A
Diane	B	B
Joleen	A	A
Jeremy	A	C
Aaron	A	A
Stacey	B	B
Kristin	A	A
Allyson	A	A
Roberto	A	A
Robin	B	C
Camilla	B	A
Esteban	A	B

Source: Marzano (1995a).

course to independently assign grades to students. The data teachers used to assign grades were exactly the same set of homework, quizzes, tests, and so on. Previously, the teachers would jointly assign grades to students using the data from the homework, quizzes, and tests. For this study, however, we asked them to assign grades without consulting each other. Both teachers also agreed that they would not consider anything other than the homework, quizzes, and tests—in other words, no nonachievement skills and abilities such as effort and behavior listed in Figure 1.1. Thus, both teachers were using exactly the same assessment information about the students to construct grades.

Again, one would assume that the grades given to students would be the same, but as Figure 1.2 illustrates, this was not the case. One student was assigned grades that differed by three letter grades (e.g., *A* vs. *D*). Two students received grades that differed by two letter grades (e.g., *A* vs. *C*), eight students' grades differed by one letter grade (e.g., *A* vs. *B*), and 15 students received the same grade from both teachers. In all, there was agreement on only 15 of 26 grades or 57.7 percent of the grades.

When presented with the information in Figure 1.2, the two teachers were amazed and wanted to discover the reasons for the differences. Upon examination, they found that they simply considered different assessments important and, consequently, weighted them differently when computing their grades. Whereas one teacher might have considered the performance task in which students demonstrated their understanding of a science concept the most important assessment of the grading period, the other might have viewed a specific homework assignment as most important.

FIGURE 1.3
Results of Studies of Grades Assigned by Team Teachers

Study #	Grade Level	Same Grade Given	1 Grade Different	2 Grades Different	3 Grades Different
1	4	65%	21%	9%	5%
2	6	71%	14%	8%	7%
3	9	45%	38%	11%	6%
4	9	53%	27%	14%	6%
5	9	74%	17%	9%	0%
6	11	47%	37%	15%	1%
7	12	55%	21%	21%	3%

Source: Marzano (1998a). Copyright © 1998 by McREL Institute. Reprinted by permission.

This lack of consistency in assigning grades by team teachers is not unusual. Figure 1.3 reports the results of seven other similar studies. The pattern exhibited in Figure 1.3 is fairly strong: Even when two teachers base grades on exactly the same information, they frequently assign different grades to students simply because they consider different homework assignments, quizzes, and tests as important.

Misinterpretation of Single Scores

The third problem with current grading practices—the misinterpretation of single scores—is probably the most insidious of the three because it is the least obvious and is built into the system teachers currently use to score classroom assessments. The problem occurs when teachers use a single score to represent student performance on a wide array of skills and abilities.

To illustrate, consider Figure 1.4, a quiz I have used to demonstrate this problem to hundreds of classroom teachers. The two sections of the quiz assess different skills and abilities. Part I—the 10 completion items—addresses multiplication; Part II—the story problem—addresses the following skills: organizing quantities into groups that do not exceed a specific quantity, reasoning deductively about quantities, and communicating mathematically.

Designing a quiz like this sets up a situation in which an overall, single score for the quiz will probably be ambiguous. To illustrate, assume that Parts I and II of the quiz are each worth 10 points, for a possible total score of 20. Now assume that three students have obtained the scores depicted in Figure 1.5. Note that the three students have very different patterns of scores on the completion items versus the word problem. Student #1 answered all of the completion items correctly, indicating competence in multiplication. However, this student received only 2 points out of 10 for the word problem, indicating difficulties in the noncomputational skills as-

FIGURE 1.4
Quiz with Sections That Assess Different Skills and Abilities

Part I

Directions: Fill in the answer for each multiplication problem.

1. $7 \times 6 =$ _____
2. $12 \times 11 =$ _____
3. $9 \times 7 =$ _____
4. $7 \times 32 =$ _____
5. $6 \times 6 =$ _____
6. $13 \times 5 =$ _____
7. $42 \times 7 =$ _____
8. $5 \times 5 =$ _____
9. $14 \times 3 =$ _____
10. $6 \times 9 =$ _____

Part II

Directions: Write your answer and show all your work on a separate piece of paper.

Treena won a seven-day scholarship worth $1,000 to the Pro Shot Basketball Camp. Round-trip travel expenses to the camp are $335 by air or $125 by train. At the camp she must choose between a week of individual instruction at $60 per day or a week of group instruction at $40 per day. Treena's food and other expenses are fixed at $45 per day. If she does not plan to spend any money other than the scholarship, what are all the choices of travel and instruction plans that she could afford to make? Explain your reasoning.

Note: Problem in Part II from Dossey, Mullis, & Jones (1993, pp. 116–117).

sessed by the word problem. The second student's pattern indicated just the opposite competencies: weak in computation, strong in problem solving. The third student exhibited a more balanced pattern.

The students have three very different profiles of scores on the two competencies assessed in the quiz, yet all three receive the same score. In short, by using "total points" as the overall indicator of how students have performed, we lose a great deal of information about students' understanding.

Problems with the use of a single, overall score on assessments are exacerbated when teachers weight sections differently. To illustrate this point to teachers, I com-

FIGURE 1.5
Scores for Three Students on the Quiz in Figure 1.4

Student	Score on 10 Completion Items	Score on Word Problem	Overall Score on Quiz
#1	10	2	12
#2	3	9	12
#3	6	6	12

Source: Marzano (1995b).

monly present the quiz in Figure 1.4, along with the following directions:

> Assume that you are going to administer the quiz to your 8th grade mathematics students tomorrow. As you can see, 10 completion items deal with computation; in the word problem, students must explain the answer they obtain. Assuming that each of the 10 completion items will count for 1 point (that is, the completion section of the quiz will count for 10 total points), how many points would you assign to the word problem? Will you assign it 10 points to make it equal to the completion section? Will you assign it more than 10 points to make it count more, or will you assign it 5 points to make it count less?

A majority of teachers assign the problem more than 10 points to make it count more than the completion items on the overall score for the quiz. Most teachers assign the problem 15 or 20 points. Some have assigned it as much as 40 points.

The weights assigned to the two sections of the quiz determine which skills and abilities are most strongly reflected in the overall score based on total points. For example, if a teacher weights the word problem twice as much as the completion items (20 points),

two-thirds of the total score will be based on students' skills in the competencies assessed by the word problem and one-third will be based on their skills in the competencies assessed by the completion items. The teacher who assigns the word problem 30 points sets up a situation in which the competencies assessed by the word problem account for 75 percent of the total score and the competencies assessed by the completion items account for 25 percent.

The three problems described here illustrate the inaccuracies and idiosyncracies of the system of classroom grading used in most schools. In fact, researchers Cross and Frary (1999) refer to the current system as the "hodgepodge" method of grading. Stated differently, teachers in U.S. schools design their own systems for classroom grading and assessment by making individual decisions about the specific factors they will consider, how they will weight these factors, and how they will combine scores on these factors in homework, quizzes, and tests. It is true that this practice provides individual teachers with a great deal of latitude and freedom. It is also true, however, that American education pays a great price for this latitude and freedom.

The Price of Our Grading Practices

Ultimately, the price we pay for the grading practices in our schools is a highly inaccurate system. At workshops on classroom grading, I frequently begin by asking educators to raise their hands if they have ever received a grade that was a "flagrantly inaccurate representation of their achievement in a course of study." Virtually all of the thousands of teachers to whom I have posed this question have raised their hands. I then ask, "How many believe that the grades you received in school were not an accurate representation of your academic achievement?" Sometimes as many as 50 percent of the educators in my workshops respond affirmatively. I find this an amazing commentary on our system of grading—even those within education have little confidence in the current system's validity.

Research on grade inflation readily shows the negative consequence of our current grading system. Specifically, there has been widespread speculation that the value of grades has decreased over the years—that the academic achievement necessary to obtain a grade of *A* now is far less than what was required a few decades ago (see Keith, 1982; Adelman, 1983; Turnbill, 1985, Bracey, 1994).

Technically, grade inflation is defined as an increase in grades without a concomitant increase in achievement (Zlomek and Svec, 1997). One frequently cited study supporting the existence of grade inflation was conducted in 1994 by the Office of Educational Research and Improvement (OERI) in the U.S. Department of Education. Based on data from a national sample of 8th grade students, researchers found that the grades of students from schools where more than 75 percent received free or reduced price lunch were significantly inflated when compared with students from schools with more affluent populations:

> How well is an *A* student in a high-poverty school doing compared to his or her counterpart in a more affluent school? These students are at a serious disadvantage, as measured by the reading and math tests given as part of the NELS:88 [National Education Longitudinal Study of 1988] data collection:

> **Reading:** Students in high-poverty schools (those where more than 75 percent of students receive free or reduced price lunch) who received mostly *A*'s in English got about the same reading score as did the *C* and *D* students in the most affluent schools.

> **Math:** The students in the high-poverty schools most closely resembled the *D* students in the most affluent schools.

> The *B* students in the schools with the highest poverty concentrations received about the same test scores as the students who received *D*'s and less than *D*'s in the schools with the lowest concentrations of poor students. The *C* students in the poorest schools got about the same test scores as the failing students in the most affluent schools. (U.S. Department of Education, 1994, pp. 3–4)

An updated version of this same study found similar results. Here is how researcher Christopher Cross reported the findings:

> In that study, data were collected on actual student grades, and then students were given the same standardized examination. As the chart [Figure 1.6] shows, *A* students in high-poverty schools score at levels on that exam that fall at about the *C–* or *D+* level of students in low-poverty schools. In my mind that equals educational fraud, plain and simple. Students in those high-poverty schools and their parents are being led to believe that they are achieving at

FIGURE 1.6
Study of 7th Graders Illustrating Grade Inflation in Low-Poverty Schools

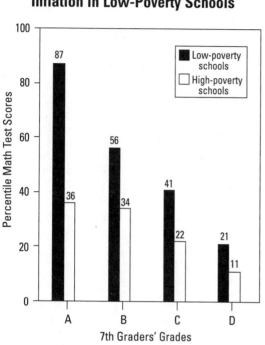

Source: Cross, C. T. (1997). Hard questions, "standard answers." *Basic Education, 42*(3), 1. Copyright © 1997 by Council for Basic Education. Reprinted by permission.

high levels when they are, in fact, not learning what they need to succeed in a wider community. Why? Because there are no standards for academic performance to indicate otherwise. (Cross, 1997, pp. 1–3)

Evidence of grade inflation has also been reported by The College Board, using SAT data:

> Since 1987, the population of students with *A* plus, *A,* and *A* minus grade-point averages has grown from 28 percent to a record 37 percent, while their SAT scores have fallen an average of 13 points on verbal and 1 point on math. This year's grade average for all SAT takers is 3.22 on a four-point scale (*A* = 4), well above the average of 3.07 in 1987. (The College Board, 1997, p. 2)

Finally, researcher Kathryn Wentzel (1991) found that most students who receive top grades in college courses (i.e., the top 12 percent) do not score at the top (i.e., the top 12 percent) in standardized tests such as the SAT.

A discussion of the research on grade inflation would not be complete without mention of the arguments against this phenomenon. Researcher Gerald Bracey (1994) asserts that educators have been too quick to accept the allegations that grades have become gradually inflated. As evidence, Bracey cites a study by researcher Leslie Wood conducted in 1994. Wood ranked the sophomores, juniors, and seniors in a high school in a large Midwestern city. The agreement between students' overall grades and their rank in class was remarkably high—the highest ranked students in each class had *A*'s, the lowest ranked students all had *D*'s. As Wood notes: "The comparison shows an amazing consistency in grades from the sophomore through the senior years. At first glance, faculty members looking at these data might feel very good about the fairness and consistency of grades in their schools" (p. 190).

However, Wood points out that there were 545 sophomores, 440 juniors, and 350 seniors. Quite obviously, the decreasing numbers of students at higher grade levels is a function of students dropping out. Commenting on Wood's study, Bracey (1994) notes:

> If one makes the reasonable assumption that those who left school had lower grade-point averages than those who stayed (data from my studies confirm this), then the grades assigned from year to year are actually declining. Stated more accurately, the same grade distribution is being applied to a student pool of ever-increasing prior achievement. (Bracey, 1994, p. 328)

In short, Wood's data suggest that as students advance in their high school years, high grades are more difficult to acquire because the competition is greater. Yet teachers continue to assign the same proportion of *A's, B's, C's,* and *D's.* In fact, Wood maintains that a sophomore with a *B–* average will probably receive a grade of *D+* for the same level of achievement by the time she is a senior. While Wood's study does not disprove the existence of grade inflation, it does indicate that the phenomenon might be more complex than originally thought.

As evidence mounts to support the intuitive suspicion that grading practices in U.S. classrooms leave much to be desired, an interesting question becomes more and more important: "How did we get to this point?" To answer this question, one must consider the history of grading practices.

A Brief History of Grades

The precise history of grading practices in American education is a matter of some debate, although most historians agree on a number of significant events. Prior to the late 1700s, students were not given grades per se. Rather, teachers gave students feedback on their performance through narrative comments. In 1780, Yale University began using a system that was probably the most identifiable precursor to the current system. Yale began providing students feedback using a four-point scale. Education historian Mark Durm (1993) notes that this scale "was the origin of the 4.0 system used by so many colleges and universities today" (p. 295). Over time, other universities began to shift from the narrative approach to more quantitative approaches. For example, William and Mary began using a numerical scale in about 1850. Harvard University's first numerical scale was initiated in 1830; it employed a 20-point scale in-

stead of a four-point scale. In 1877, Harvard began classifying students into "Divisions."

Division 1: 90 or more on a scale of 100
Division 2: 75–90
Division 3: 60–74
Division 4: 50–59
Division 5: 40–49
Division 6: below 40

It is not hard to see the beginnings of the *A, B, C* approach used in the Harvard divisions. In fact, it wasn't too long after Harvard began using divisions that Mount Holyoke College started using letter grades. More precisely, in 1897 Mount Holyoke initiated the following system:

A: Excellent = equivalent to percents 95–100
B: Good = equivalent to percents 85–94
C: Fair = equivalent to percents 76–84
D: Passed = barely equivalent to percent 75
E: Failed = below 75

For the most part, this 100-year tradition is still in place today. In a study involving over 1,700 school districts, Robinson and Craver (1989) reported the results depicted in Figures 1.7, 1.8, 1.9, and 1.10.

As illustrated in Figures 1.7 through 1.10, the vast majority of districts reported using letter grades. Specifically, about 80 percent of schools use letter grades from the 4th grade on. Percentage scores are the second most frequent method of reporting student achievement with about 25 percent of schools using the format from the 4th grade on. The use of satisfactory/unsatisfactory scores and item checklists are far less common except in kindergarten and primary grades. Finally, a 1998 study con-

FIGURE 1.7
Percentage of Schools Using Letter Grades at Various Grade Levels

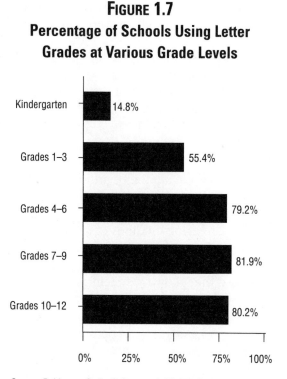

Source: Robinson, G. E., & Craver, J. M. (1989). *Assessing and grading student achievement* (p. 26). Arlington, VA: Educational Research Service. Copyright © 1989 Educational Research Service. Reprinted by permission.

FIGURE 1.8
Percentage of Schools Using Percentage Grades at Various Grade Levels

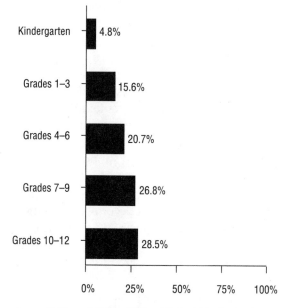

Source: Robinson & Craver (1989, p. 26). Copyright © 1989 Educational Research Service. Reprinted by permission.

ducted by The College Board reported that out of 3,113 high schools responding to a survey, 91 percent reported using *A–F* or an equivalent numeric grading scheme. Clearly, overall grades are a central aspect of education in the United States.

The Importance of a Common Vocabulary

The final issue we will consider in this chapter is the need for a common vocabulary about grades. Although this issue might not seem immediately relevant to solving the problems surrounding grading practices, a common understanding of terminology is key to advancement in any field (Clark & Clark, 1977). Applying this principle to grading, one can conclude that using the terminology of grading more precisely will increase our understanding of it, whereas our casual use of terms such as grades, marks, and assessments might add to our confusion. Fortunately, these terms have relatively specific meanings if we consult the writings of researchers and theorists such as James Terwilliger (1989), Ken O'Connor (1995), Rick Stiggins (1994, 1997), Grant Wiggins (1994, 1996, 1998), and James McMillan (1997, in press). The following terms and definitions will be used throughout this book:

Assessment: Vehicles for gathering information about students' achievement or behavior.

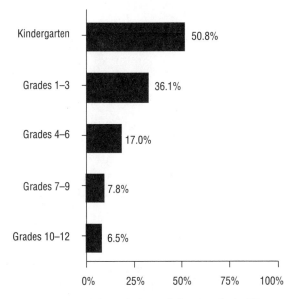

FIGURE 1.9
Percentage of Schools Using Satisfactory/Unsatisfactory Grades at Various Grade Levels

Source: Robinson & Craver (1989, p. 27). Copyright © 1989 Educational Research Service. Reprinted by permission.

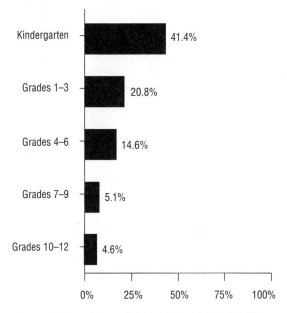

FIGURE 1.10
Percentage of Schools Using Item Checklists at Various Grade Levels

Source: Robinson & Craver (1989, p. 29). Copyright © 1989 Educational Research Service. Reprinted by permission.

Evaluation: The process of making judgments about the level of students' understanding or performance.

Measurement: The assignment of marks based on an explicit set of rules.

Score(s): The number(s) or letter(s) assigned to an assessment via the process of measurement. The terms *mark* and *score* are commonly used synonymously.

Grade(s): The number(s) or letter(s) reported at the end of a set period of time as a summary statement of evaluations made of students.

Conclusion

Today's system of classroom grading is at least 100 years old and has little or no re-

search to support its continuation. At least three inherent problems make that system highly ineffective: (1) it allows, and even encourages, individual teachers to include, at their own discretion, different nonachievement factors in the assignment of grades; (2) it allows individual teachers to differentially weight assessment; and (3) it mixes different types of knowledge and skills into single scores on assessments.

This book is designed to help educators solve all three of these problems. It is important to note, however, that solutions will vary from district to district and school to school. From the variety of approaches provided here, individual districts, schools, and teachers can select those solutions that best meet their goals, needs, and resources.

What Are Grades For?

This book is about designing classroom grading systems that are both precise and efficient. One of the first steps to this end is to clarify the basic purpose of grades. How a school or district defines the purpose of grades dictates much of the form and function of grades.

Purposes of Grades

Measurement experts such as Peter Airasian (1994) explain that educators use grades primarily (1) for administrative purposes, (2) to give students feedback about their progress and achievement, (3) to provide guidance to students about future course work, (4) to provide guidance to teachers for instructional planning, and (5) to motivate students.

Administrative Purposes

For at least several decades, grades have served a variety of administrative functions (Wrinkle, 1947), most dealing with district-level decisions about students, including

- Student matriculation and retention.
- Placement when students transfer from one school to another.
- Student entrance into college.

Airasian (1994) further explains that "administratively, schools need grades to determine such things as a pupil's rank in class, credits for graduation, and suitability for promotion to the next level" (p. 283).

Research indicates that some districts explicitly make note of the administrative function of grades. For example, in a study of school board manuals, district guidelines, and handbooks for teaching, researchers Susan Austin and Richard McCann (1992) found the explicit mention of administration as a basic purpose for grades in 7 percent of school board documents, 10 percent of district guidelines, and 4 percent of handbooks for teachers. Finally, in a survey conducted by The College Board (1998), over 81 percent of the schools reported using grades for administrative purposes.

Feedback About Student Achievement

One of the more obvious purposes for grades is to provide feedback about student achievement. Studies have consistently shown support for this purpose. For example, in 1976, Simon and Bellanca reported that both educators and noneducators perceived providing information about student achievement as the primary purpose of grading. In a 1989 study of high school teachers, Stiggins, Frisbie, and Griswold reported that this grading function—which they refer to as the information function—was highly valued by teachers. Finally, the study by Austin and McCann (1992) found that 25 percent of school board documents, 45 percent of district documents, and 65 percent of teacher documents mentioned reporting student achievement as a basic purpose of grades.

Guidance

When used for guidance purposes, grades help counselors provide direction for students (Wrinkle, 1947; Terwilliger, 1971). Specifically, counselors use grades to recommend to individual students courses they should or should not take and schools and occupations they might consider (Airasian, 1994). Austin and McCann (1992) found that 82 percent of school board documents, 40 percent of district documents, and 38 percent of teacher documents identified guidance as an important purpose of grades.

Instructional Planning

Teachers also use grades to make initial decisions about student strengths and weaknesses in order to group them for instruction. Grading as a tool for instructional planning is not commonly mentioned by measurement experts. However, the Austin and McCann (1992) study reported that 44 percent of school board documents, 20 percent of district documents, and 10 percent of teacher documents emphasized this purpose.

Motivation

Those who advocate using grades to motivate students assume that they encourage students to try harder both from negative and positive perspectives. On the negative side, receiving a low grade is believed to motivate students to try harder. On the positive side, it is assumed that receiving a high grade will motivate students to continue or renew their efforts.

As discussed later in this chapter, some educators object strongly to using grades as motivators. Rightly or wrongly, however, this purpose is manifested in some U.S. schools. For example, Austin and McCann (1992) found that 7 percent of school board documents, 15 percent of district-level documents, and 10 percent of teacher documents emphasized motivation as a purpose for grades.

Which Is the Most Important Purpose?

According to the research cited in the previous sections, each of the five purposes for grading has some support from educators. A useful question is which of the five purposes is the most important or, more generally stated, what is the relative impor-

FIGURE 2.1
Ranking of Importance of Five Purposes for Grading
From Austin and McCann Study and Author's Informal Survey

Purposes	Austin and McCann			Informal Survey		Average Rank
	Board Documents	District Documents	School Documents	Teachers	Administrators	
Administration	4	5	4	3	2	3.6
Feedback About Student Achievement	3	1	1	1	1	1.4
Guidance	1	2	2	5	3	2.6
Instructional Planning	2	3	3	4	5	3.4
Motivation	4	4	3	2	4	3.4

Key: 1 = high, 5 = low

tance of the five purposes? Figure 2.1 depicts the results of the Austin and McCann (1992) study compared with an informal survey I undertook in preparing this book. (That survey is discussed in depth in Chapter 7.) If one uses the average rank (the last column) from the two studies as the criterion, Figure 2.1 indicates that using grades to provide feedback about student achievement should be considered the primary function of grades. Guidance is ranked second, instructional planning and motivation are tied for third, and administration is last. However, to obtain the most accurate picture of the opinions about the various purpose of grades, it is important to notice the variation in responses in Figure 2.1: whereas teachers in my informal survey ranked guidance as the least important, board-level documents ranked it as the most important. Whereas district-level documents ranked use of grades for adminis-

trative purposes last, administrators in my informal survey ranked it second.

In short, there is no clear pattern of preference across the various sources except for the importance of feedback. Consequently, schools and districts must undertake their own studies of teachers and administrators regarding the purpose of grades. Again, use of an informal survey with teachers and administrators is discussed in depth in Chapter 7.

The Issue of Reference

Another issue to address when developing a coherent grading system is the point of reference from which grades are interpreted. Three primary reference points are commonly used to interpret grades: (1) a predetermined distribution, (2) an established set of objectives, and (3) progress of individual students.

Reference to a Predetermined Distribution

Assigning grades based on a predetermined distribution can be thought of as a "norm-referenced" approach to grading. The concept of norm-referencing is so embedded in educational practice that it is worth discussing in some detail. Most educators are familiar with the term as it relates to standardized tests. For example, scores on tests like the *Iowa Tests of Basic Skills* commonly are reported as percentile ranks. Results for a particular student on the reading comprehension section of a standardized test might be reported as the 73rd percentile, meaning that the score the student received was higher than 73 percent of the scores received by other students. These "other students" to which the sample student's score is compared are referred to as the "norming group." With standardized tests, the norming group is usually assumed to be students across the country at the same age/grade level. Additionally, it is commonly assumed that the scores of the norming group, when arranged in order of magnitude, are distributed in a "bell curve."

The technical name for the "bell curve" is the "normal distribution." As depicted in Figure 2.2, the normal distribution is quite symmetrical, which allows mathematicians and statisticians to make a wide variety of predictions based on it. You might recall from statistics or measurement classes that about 68 percent of the scores in a normal distribution will fall within one standard deviation above and below the mean; about 95 percent of the scores will fall within two standard deviations above and below the mean, and almost 100 percent of the scores will fall within three standard deviations above and below the mean.

The concept of normal distribution has had a profound effect on educational practice—and, indeed, on Western society. The mathematical equation for the normal distribution was formulated as early as 1733 by Abraham de Moivre (1667–1754). Its critical importance to probability theory was later articulated by mathematicians Pierre de Laplace (1749–1827) and Carl Friedrich Gauss (1777–1855). Today, Gauss is commonly thought of as the father of the normal distribution. In fact, so compelling were his writings about the characteristics and applications of the normal distribution, that it is frequently referred to as the "Gaussian distribution."

The wide use of the normal distribution in education stems from the fact that many physical and psychological phenomena adhere to it. For example, Figure 2.3 depicts the distribution of the height in inches of young Englishmen called upon for military service in 1939 as well as the distribution of IQ scores of 2,835 children ages 6 and 11 years randomly selected from London schools. For illustrative purposes both are plotted on a common axis.

Figure 2.3 dramatically illustrates that many characteristics do take the shape of a normal distribution when they are arranged in order of magnitude. Perhaps this is why many prominent researchers assume that the normal distribution can and should be used to describe student achievement. Among the most prominent are Arthur Jensen, Richard Heurnstein, and Charles Murray. Jensen is perhaps most well known for his book *Bias in Mental Testing* (1980). In it he argues that because aptitude is distributed normally, educators and psychologists should generally expect grades (or scores on any educational test) to conform to a normal distribution. Jensen notes that a tendency for scores to

FIGURE 2.2
The Normal Distribution (Bell Curve)

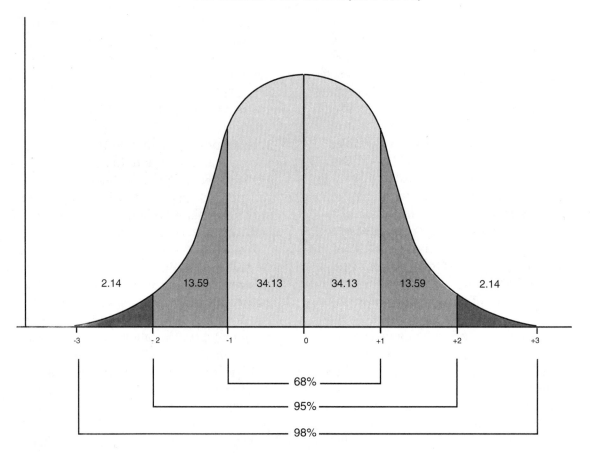

take the form of the normal distribution is so strong that it occurs even when tests are designed in such a way as to avoid a normal distribution. He offers the following anecdote about Alfred Binet designing the first practical intelligence test:

> Historically, the first workable mental tests were constructed without any thought of the normal distribution, and yet the distribution of scores was roughly normal. Alfred Binet, in making the first practical intelligence test, selected items only according to how well they discriminated between younger and older children, and between children of the same age who were judged bright or dull by

their teachers, and by how well the items correlated with one another. He also tried to get a variety of items so that item-specific factors of ability or knowledge would not be duplicated. . . . and he tried to find items rather evenly graded in difficulty. . . . Under these conditions it turned out, in fact, that the distribution of raw scores (number of items correct) within any one-year age interval was roughly normal. (Jensen, 1980, p. 71)

Richard Heurnstein and Charles Murray wrote the popular book *The Bell Curve* (1994). In this controversial work, the authors make a case not only that intelligence is distributed normally, but that it is

FIGURE 2.3
Distribution of Height in Inches of Englishmen and IQ Scores of Young Children

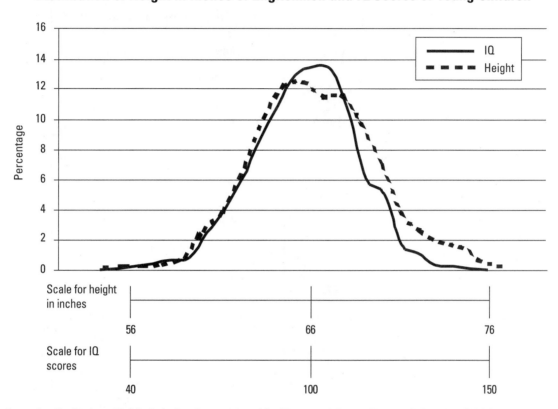

Source for distribution of height in inches: Data reported by Harrison, Weiner, Tanner, & Barnicot (1964).

Source for distribution of IQ scores: Data reported by Burt (1957).

a prime determinant of differences in factors such as income level, parenting ability, success in school, and virtually every social indicator of success. Of course, this position has rather strong negative implications for members of certain socioeconomic strata.

Because a teacher uses the normal distribution as a basis for grading does not necessarily mean that he or she agrees with the assertions of Jensen or Heurnstein and Murray. However, by using the bell curve as the reference point for grading, a teacher is implicitly assuming that the performance of students should or will approximate the

bell curve. Consequently, the teacher forces a set of scores or set of grades into a normal distribution. To illustrate, assume that during a nine-week grading period students in a given course accumulated the points depicted in Figure 2.4.

The teacher would arrange these scores in order from the lowest to the highest. Then, using knowledge of the normal distribution, the teacher would partition the scores into groups and then assign grades (shown in Figure 2.5).

From the discussion of Figure 2.2 we know that certain percentages of scores in

FIGURE 2.4
Total Points Earned by 30 Students During a Nine-Week Grading Period

Student	Points	Student	Points
Bob	205	Alexander	205
Jana	293	Steve	271
Todd	230	Mark	204
Christine	246	Lorraine	250
Carmen	284	Robert	247
Ashley	242	Cliff	297
Joe	245	Luigi	254
Mike	270	Asunta	213
Louie	251	Naomi	233
Cliff	257	Jefferson	256
Julia	266	Lee	247
Christy	257	Willie	281
Joseph	266	Carol	275
Jennifer	237	Jose	243
Brian	253	Nilda	257

a normal distribution fall between certain intervals above and below the average score. Specifically, scores within a normal distribution can be organized into the following six categories:

1. About 2 percent of the scores will be 2 or more standard deviations above the average score.

2. About 14 percent of the scores will be between 1 and 2 standard deviations above the average score.

3. About 34 percent of the scores will be between the average score and 1 standard deviation above the average score.

4. About 34 percent of the scores will be between the average score and 1 standard deviation below the average score.

5. About 14 percent of the scores will be between 1 and 2 standard deviations below the average score.

6. About 2 percent of the scores will be 2 or more standard deviations below the average score.

Knowing this, a teacher can divide students' scores into six intervals and then assign grades based on them. Specifically, the teacher will allow only about 2 percent of the students to be in the top category, 14

FIGURE 2.5
Grades Assigned to 30 Students During a Nine-Week Grading Period Using the Normal Distribution

Score	204	205	205	213	230	233	237	242	243	245	246	247	247	250	251	253	254	256	257	257	257	266	266	270	271	275	281	284	293	297
Percentage expected based on the normal distribution	2%	14%				34%										34%										14%				2%
Expected number out of 30 students	1	4				10										10										4				1
Assigned grade	F	D				C										B										A				A

percent in the second category, and so on. Therefore, scores identified in the top 2 percent will be assigned to the top category, the next 14 percent of the scores to the second highest category, and so on.

Finally, the teacher would assign letter grades to each category. In Figure 2.5, the teacher has assigned a letter grade of *A* to the top two categories, a grade of *B* to the third highest category, and so on.

It is important to note that the normal distribution is not the only distribution that can be the point of reference for assigning grades. For example, one teacher I worked with told me that she always uses the following scheme to assign grades:

A's: 25%
B's: 50%
C's: 20%
D's: 5%

This practice, although somewhat more benevolent than the use of the normal distribution, still predetermines the percentages of various grades; the teacher is simply using a different distribution to determine these percentages. Occasionally, the distribution that is to form the basis for grades is made explicit in school or district policy. For example, in their study of grading practices, Austin and McCann report one district's policy:

> There should be about as many marks of 3.5 or higher as there are pupils in a group with IQ's of 120 or above. There should be about as many marks of *F* (1.0 to 1.5) as there are pupils with IQ's of 95 or less. It is expected that the number of marks at the 3.5 level or higher, and at the 1.5 level or lower, may have a variance of 25 percent of the pupils in the IQ groups of 120 and up, and 95 and below. (1992, p. 10)

Reference to a Set of Learning Objectives

Specific learning objectives are another common point of reference for grades. Many measurement experts strongly endorse this approach. For example, James

Terwilliger (1989) notes that "grading should be directly linked to an explicitly defined set of instructional goals . . ." (p. 15). This approach is commonly thought of as a "criterion-referenced" approach to grading, as opposed to the norm-referenced approach described previously.

Again, you are probably familiar with the term "criterion-referenced" as it relates to tests designed to assess student achievement on state standards. In such cases, the criterion is a specific score sometimes referred to as a "cut score." Students who do not obtain a score equal to or greater than the "cut score" are assumed not to have mastered the content at the requisite level. Of course, the key to designing such a test is to ensure that it contains items that students will answer correctly if they have a mastery of the content, but will answer incorrectly if they do not. Unfortunately, it is very difficult to design tests with truly valid "cut scores" (see Livingston, 1982).

Mathematics educators Warner Esty and Anne Teppo (1992) have described how they use a criterion-referenced system as the basis for grades in mathematics classes. They explain their system in the context of a unit on the concept of *function*. Before the unit begins, they clearly describe what the grades *A*, *B*, *C*, and so on will represent. Then, when the unit begins, they communicate this scale of understanding to the students. Each quiz, test, homework assignment, and so on is then graded using this scale. A *C* on the first quiz of the grading period indicates to a student that "at the present time" your understanding of the concept of a function is at the *C* level. The final grade for a student is his or her level of understanding of the concept at the end of a grading period.

This last point is very important to the criterion-referenced approach to grading.

Because the target is a specific level of learning, the final grade is commonly considered the level of learning the student has reached by the end of the unit of instruction. This makes good sense within a criterion-referenced system. Stated negatively, it would make little sense to combine all test scores for a given student (by computing an average score for example) during a unit, because this might penalize the student for his lack of knowledge at the beginning of the unit. The driving force behind criterion-referenced grading is to ascertain the extent to which students reach a specific level of knowledge or skill in a specific learning outcome at the end of a grading period.

Reference to Knowledge Gain

As the name implies, reference to knowledge gain uses individual student learning as the basis for grading. In this approach, the point of reference for each student is the level of skill or understanding at which the student begins the grading period. Stated differently, each student's entry level of knowledge is his or her unique point of reference. Each student's grade then, is based on how much he or she progresses beyond the initial level of knowledge or skill. The logic behind this approach is that students should not be compared to one another but, rather, to the amount of progress they can legitimately be expected to make. One challenge in this approach is to design a scale that can accommodate the different beginning points of reference for each student. Following is a sample of the types of scales that must be used in this approach.

A = Exceptional effort and improvement in the student's ability

B = Good effort; improvement exceeds expectations

C = Adequate effort; improvement consistent with level of effort and ability

D = Little improvement, but some evidence of effort

F = Little or no improvement; no effort

As this example illustrates, when a student's entry-level knowledge is used as the reference point for grades, teachers commonly include these factors: (1) understanding of and skill in the content, (2) effort, and (3) aptitude. The highest grades are given to students who exhibit exceptional effort and improvement beyond what is expected of them (i.e., beyond what is expected for their level of aptitude).

The Position of This Book

Although there is no right way or wrong way to design grades, there are ways that fit best with a given set of assumptions or beliefs. This book is based on two assumptions:

1. The most important purpose for grades is to provide information or feedback to students and parents.

2. The best referencing system for grading is content-specific learning goals: a criterion-referenced approach.

Research unquestionably supports the importance of feedback to specific learning goals. To illustrate, after reviewing 7,827 studies on learning and instruction, researcher John Hattie (1992) reported that providing students with specific information about their standing in terms of particular objectives increased their achievement by 37 percentile points. To dramatize the implications of this research, assume that two students of equal ability are in the same class learning the same content. Also assume that they take a test on the content before beginning instruction and that both receive a score that puts their knowledge of the content at the 50th percentile. Four weeks go by and the students receive exactly the same instruction, the same assignments, and so on. However, one student receives systematic feedback in terms of specific learning goals; the other does not. After four weeks, the two students take another test. Everything else being equal, the student who received the systematic feedback obtained a score that was 34 percentile points higher than the score of the student who had not received feedback. It was this dramatic finding that led Hattie to remark: "The most powerful single innovation that enhances achievement is feedback. The simplest prescription for improving education must be 'dollops of feedback' " (p. 9).

The Case Against Having Any Grades at All

Before concluding this general discussion of grades, let's look at a final topic: doing away with any form of quantitative feedback. More specifically, the practice of providing students with quantitative feedback about their knowledge or skill has been strongly criticized by a few zealous and, unfortunately, persuasive individuals. Education writer Alfie Kohn is perhaps the most well known of this group. In a series of publications, Kohn asserts that almost all forms of grading should be abolished. His popular book *Punished by Rewards: The Trouble with Gold Stars, Incentive Plans, A's, Praise and Other Bribes* (1993) begins with an impassioned case against the use of rewards to motivate students. Kohn explains that American education is ostensibly trapped in a pattern of trying to bribe students into achievement.

> . . . Regardless of the political persuasion or social class, whether a Fortune 500 CEO, or a preschool teacher, we are immersed in this doctrine; it is as American as rewarding someone with apple pie.
>
> To induce students to learn, we present stickers, stars, certificates, awards, trophies, memberships in elite societies, and, above all, grades. (Kohn, 1993, p. 11)

Kohn blames this pattern of behavior on what he calls "pop behaviorism," which, he asserts, permeates our culture and our educational system: "Pop behaviorism is perpetuated through the example of other significant individuals in our lives, too, including teachers and powerful people in the workplace" (p. 15). For Kohn, behaviorism so permeates the culture of education that we are literally unaware of it.

To counteract the negative influence of behaviorism on American education, Kohn cites a number of studies indicating that rewards do not positively influence behavior. For example, rewards are not good motivators in helping people lose weight, quit smoking, or use seat belts. He also cites research indicating that rewards do not improve performance on cognitive tasks. He places heavy emphasis on a dissertation by Louise Miller, who arranged a series of drawings of faces so pairs of identical and nearly identical images would be flashed on the screen. Nine-year-olds were then asked to differentiate between identical and nonidentical faces. Some of the students were paid when they succeeded; others were not. As Kohn explains, Miller

> brought 72 nine-year-olds into her laboratory one at a time and challenged them to tell the two faces apart. Some of the

boys were paid when they succeeded, others were simply told each time whether or not they were correct. (1993, p. 42)

To the surprise of the researcher, the performance of the group that was paid was inferior to that of the group that was not.

In a later work entitled *Beyond Discipline: From Compliance to Community* (1996) Kohn summarizes the research on rewards:

> At least two dozen studies have shown that when people are promised a reward for doing a reasonably challenging task— or for doing it well—they tend to do inferior work compared with people who are given the same task without being promised any reward at all. Other research has shown that one of the least effective ways to get people to change their behavior (quit smoking, lose weight, use their seatbelts, and so on) is to offer them an incentive for doing so. The promise of a reward is sometimes not just ineffective but counterproductive—that is, worse than doing nothing at all. (p. 33)

Finally, in a 1999 article entitled "From Grading to Degrading," Kohn asserts that

• Grades tend to reduce students' interest in learning itself.
• Grades tend to reduce students' preference for challenging tasks.
• Grades tend to reduce the quality of students' thinking. (p. 39)

Based on his analysis of research on rewards—particularly monetary rewards—Kohn calls for significant changes in grading practices within education. Specifically, in *Punished by Rewards*, Kohn (1993, pp. 208–209) recommends that educators

1. Limit the number of assignments for which you give a letter grade.

2. Do not grade assignments using an *A/B/C/D/F* scale. Rather, use a scale like the following: check-plus/check/check-minus.

3. Reduce the number of possible grades to two: *A* and incomplete.

4. Never grade students when they are still learning something.

5. Never grade for effort.

6. Never grade on a curve.

7. Bring students in on the evaluation process as much as possible.

Some of Kohn's recommendations have merit—particularly 4, 6, and 7. Others, however, are questionable, at best, and downright dangerous, at worst. I believe Kohn's argument suffers from four primary weaknesses or misconceptions.

First, Kohn does not adequately address the complexities surrounding the issues of assessing and evaluating human learning. Stated differently, he ignores the research on the inappropriate and appropriate uses of assessment as a tool in the learning process. This book is an attempt to articulate the very issues that Kohn has ignored.

Second, Kohn does not accurately interpret the influence of behaviorism on education today. Specifically, he interprets as behavioristic a wide variety of educational practices that have little or nothing to do with behaviorism. Psychologist John Anderson explains that this is a common trap:

> Modern educational writers assume that the behaviorist approach to education has been a failure, although little hard evidence has been cited. Recent writings have tended to generalize the perceived failure of the behaviorist program to the conclusion that any program that attempts to analyze a skill into components will fail. (1995, p. 396)

Anderson speaks out strongly against what he considers educators' lack of understanding of the research in cognitive psychology. Speaking specifically about a review of the research in cognitive psychology by a prominent educational researcher (i.e., Shepard, 1991), Anderson notes: "In a gross misreading of the cognitive psychology literature, it has been claimed that modern cognitive research has proved that much componential analysis is in error" (p. 396).

Third, Kohn appears to misinterpret the research on grading, perhaps because he confuses rewards with feedback. Although it is true that tangible rewards have little effect on achievement, feedback has a strong and straightforward relationship to achievement. As mentioned previously, in a review of 7,827 studies in education, Hattie (1992) found that accurate feedback to students can increase their level of knowledge and understanding by 37 percentile points.

Finally, Kohn does not address the rather extensive body of research on rewards that contradicts his basic thesis. A basic premise for Kohn is that the rewards inhibit intrinsic motivation. However, in a review of 96 experimental studies, researchers Judy Cameron and W. David Pierce (1994) note: "Results indicate that, overall, reward does not decrease intrinsic motivation. When interaction effects are examined, findings show that verbal praise produces an increase in intrinsic motivation. The only negative effect appears when expected tangible rewards are given to individuals simply for doing a task. Under these conditions, there is a minimal negative effect on intrinsic motivation . . ." (p. 363). Speaking specifically about grades, researcher David Berliner explains:

> In fact, the evidence is persuasive that grades do motivate students to learn more in a given subject area. . . . The judi-

cious use of grades that are tied to objective performance, as in mastery and some other instructional programs, appears to be related to increased achievement and positive student attitudes. (1984, p. 70)

Research offers strong support for grades and others forms of feedback (even rewards) as useful tools for learning. Unfortunately, because of a great many misconceptions about their use they have fallen out of favor with some educators.

Conclusion

In this chapter we've looked at the basic purpose of and the point of reference for grades. Out of five potential purposes, feedback was identified as the most important. Out of three possible points of reference, specific learning outcomes was deemed the most compatible with feedback as a purpose. Finally, we examined arguments against the use of grades, particularly those proposed by Alfie Kohn.

∃ What Should Be Included in Grades?

I n Chapter 2 we saw that student feedback should be the central purpose for grades, given its importance in the learning process. To be effective, feedback must be specific. For the purpose of classroom grades, teachers must make their grading criteria explicit. On the surface, this seems straightforward: teachers obviously will use students' knowledge of content as the basis for grades. However, research illustrates that this seemingly simple matter is actually quite complex. Specifically, in a series of studies, Rick Stiggins and his colleagues (Stiggins, Frisbie & Griswold, 1989; Stiggins & Conklin, 1992) found that teachers commonly include many and various factors when constructing classroom grades. In fact, this was the first of the three problems about grading practices introduced in Chapter 1. In this chapter, we discuss four factors that teachers commonly include in grading: academic achievement, effort, behavior, and attendance.

Academic Achievement

By far, academic achievement is the most commonly cited factor that should be included in grades (Stiggins et al., 1989; Stiggins & Conklin, 1992). In its simplest form, the rationale might be that "those who learn more should receive higher grades." Rick Stiggins elaborates on this point:

> Schools exist to promote student achievement. In that sense, it is the most valued outcome of schools. If students achieve, schools are seen as working effectively. Grades are supposed to reflect a student's level of success in learning the required material. (1994, p. 369)

When teachers use academic achievement as a grading criterion, they assign grades in a manner proportional to the amount of content students learn. If they learn a great deal of content, students receive a high grade; if they learn very little content, they receive a low grade.

Effort

As described by Stiggins (1997, p. 412), the logic behind using effort as a grading criterion might be stated as: students who try harder receive a higher grade than those who achieve at the same level but put less effort into their work. In the classrooms they studied, researchers Dan Wright and Martin Wise (1988) found that academic achievement and effort considered together account for about 80 percent of what differentiates one grade from another (technically, 80 percent of the variance in grades). That these two factors were the primary criteria teachers used to assign grades was also reported by researcher Susan Brookhart (1994) in a major review of 19 studies, and in a study by Frary, Cross, and Weber (1993) of 536 high school teachers.

What do teachers use as evidence of student effort? Based on research, one factor appears to be the extent to which students complete classroom tasks in a timely and appropriate fashion. To illustrate, researcher Susan Brookhart (1993) provided teachers with various grading scenarios and asked them to react. Consider the following:

Scenario #1
In your 7th grade social studies class, report card grades were based on quizzes, tests, and an out-of-class project, which counted as 25 percent of the grade. Terry obtained an *A* average on his quizzes and tests, but has not turned in his project despite frequent reminders. In this situation, you would . . .

Scenario #2
You teach English to a class of 9th graders with varying ability levels. During this grading period, the students' grades are based on quizzes, tests, and homework assignments that involve working out exercises. Kelly has not turned in any homework assignments despite your frequent reminders. His grades on the quizzes have ranged from 65 percent to 75 percent, and he received a D on each of the tests. In this situation, you would . . . (Brookhart, 1993, p. 131)

For scenario #1, 99 percent of the teachers Brookhart polled considered the tardiness of Terry's project an indicator of lack of effort and lowered his grade (although teachers differed in terms of how much they lowered the grade). The same phenomenon occurred in scenario #2. Of the teachers polled, 86 percent considered Kelly's poor record of turning in homework as a lack of effort and gave him a final grade of *F*.

Behavior

Teachers generally interpret behavior as the extent to which students follow classroom rules and procedures, and, according to research, they often include it as a factor in grades. For example, in a study of 307 middle and high school teachers, Cross and Frary (1999) found that 37 percent said they do so. Some studies have demonstrated that behavior is weighted quite heavily as a grading criterion. In fact, Leiter and Brown (1983) found that in the primary grades, behavior was the chief criterion: "By far the strongest force in shaping grading . . . is the teacher's perceptions of student conformity with the teacher's preferred attitude and behavior patterns" (p. 18).

Attendance

It is probably safe to say that attendance is used far less as a grading criterion than achievement, effort, or behavior. However, some districts and schools mandate it (see Robinson & Craver, 1989). Attendance is most commonly used to lower grades only. If a student is absent or tardy beyond a certain number of times, the grade is lowered. Perfect attendance and punctuality, however, do not increase a student's grade.

Which Factor Is Most Important?

Ultimately, deciding which factors to include in grades is a value-driven decision. However, research does provide some rather strong guidelines. Figure 3.1 summarizes the findings on grading criteria from four of the most well-known studies on grading:

1. Perhaps the most extensive study conducted on grading—a 1989 survey of grading policies in 1,733 districts—was reported by Robinson and Craver.
2. Austin and McCann (1992) analyzed grading policies in 116 school board and district-level policy documents and 116 school-level documents, such as policy documents produced by science departments or mathematics departments.
3. Nava and Loyd surveyed 829 elementary and secondary teachers in 1992 from 18 different districts to ascertain their grading policies.
4. In 1989, Stiggins, Frisbie, and Griswold conducted in-depth case studies of grading practices of 15 high school teachers.

The primacy of academic achievement as a grading criterion is clear from Figure 3.1—it received the most emphasis in all four studies:

- 84.4 percent of the districts in the Robinson and Craver (1989) study.
- 79 percent of school board and district documents and 99 percent of school-level documents in the Austin and McCann (1992) study.
- 52 percent of the criteria identified as most important to grades addressed

achievement in the Nava and Loyd (1992) study.
- 100 percent of the teachers surveyed in the Stiggins, Frisbie, and Griswold (1989) study.

The ranking of the other four factors is not as readily apparent in Figure 3.1, although one could make a case that effort is second because it was mentioned by

- 28.5 percent of the districts in the Robinson and Craver study.
- 27 percent of school board and district documents and 44 percent of school-level documents in the Austin and McCann study.
- 8 percent of the criteria in the Nava and Loyd study.
- 87 percent of the teachers in the Stiggins, Frisbie, and Griswold study.

My position in this book is that academic achievement is the primary factor on which grades should be based. However, given the relatively broad acceptance of effort and the less strong but still significant support for behavior as well as attendance, I also present techniques for keeping records on these factors so that they can be included as criteria if a teacher, school, or district so chooses.

What Is Academic Achievement?

The question of what exactly academic achievement is might sound like one with an obvious answer. However, I have found that educators provide some surprisingly different answers. In general, they tend to include three categories of information and skill in their definitions: (1) subject-specific content, (2) thinking and reasoning skills, and (3) general communication skills.

FIGURE 3.1
Summary of Findings on Grading Criteria from Four Studies

Study	Robinson & Craver, 1989	Austin & McCann, 1992	Nava & Loyd, 1992	Stiggins, Frisbie, & Griswold, 1989
Method and Population	Survey of policies in 1,733 districts	Analysis of 116 school board and district documents and 116 school-level documents	Survey of 829 elementary and secondary teach-ers in 18 districts	Case studies of 15 high school teachers
Academic Achievement	Percentage of districts that include achievement as grading criterion by grade levels: K: 54.6 1–3: 89.1 4–6: 91.2 7–9: 93.1 10–12: 94.0 Average: **84.4**	• 79% of school board and dis-trict documents include achieve-ment as a grad-ing criterion • 99% of school -level documents	52% of the criteria identified as most important to grades addressed achievement factors	100% of the teachers used achievement as a grading criterion
Aptitude	Percentage of districts including aptitude: K: 13.1 1–3: 9.8 4–6: 7.6 7–9: 6.0 10–12: 4.9 Average: **8.3**	No information	4% of the criteria addressed aptitude factors	50% of the teachers used aptitude as a grading criterion
Effort	Percentage of districts including effort: K: 25.9 1–3: 25.7 4–6: 26.0 7–9: 31.7 10–12: 33.4 Average: **28.5**	• 27% of school board and dis-trict documents • 44% of school-level documents	8% of the criteria addressed effort factors	87% of the teachers used effort as a grading criterion
Behavior	Percentage of districts including attitude and behavior: K: 4.3 1–3: 3.9 4–6: 4.1 7–9: 6.5 10–12: 8.2 Average: **5.4**	• 11% of school board and dis-trict documents • 21% of school-level documents	8% of the criteria addressed attitude and behavior factors	13% of the teachers used attitude and be-havior as a grading criterion
Attendance	Percentage of districts including attendance: K: 6.3 1–3: 7.0 4–6: 7.1 7–9: 13.6 10–12: 17.4 Average: **10.3**	• 14% of school board documents • 17% of school-level documents	4% of the criteria addressed atten-dance factors	No information

Subject-Specific Content

As the name implies, subject-specific content involves information and skill that is *unique* to a specific discipline. It is generally assumed that teachers who use the same textbook provide students instruction on the same subject-specific content. However, research shows that individual teachers exercise so much decision-making power over the actual content covered that no one is exactly sure what students are exposed to. For example, studies (Doyle, 1992; Stodolsky, 1989; Yoon, Burstein, & Gold, n.d.) indicate that even when highly structured textbooks are the basis for a curriculum, teachers commonly make independent and idiosyncratic decisions about what to emphasize, add, and delete. This practice creates huge holes in the continuum of content to which students are exposed. In *The Learning Gap*, Stevenson and Stigler (1992) observed the following:

> Daunted by the length of most textbooks and knowing that the children's future teachers will be likely to return to the material, American teachers often omit some topics. Different topics are omitted by different teachers thereby making it impossible for the children's later teachers to know what has been covered at earlier grades—they cannot be sure what their students know and do not know. (p. 140)

At a more anecdotal level, E. D. Hirsch, author of *Cultural Literacy* (1987), makes this same point in his book *The Schools We Need: Why We Don't Have Them*:

> We know, of course, that there exists no national curriculum, but we assume, quite reasonably, that agreement has been reached locally regarding what should be taught to children at each grade level—if not within the whole district, then certainly within an individual school. . . . But . . . the idea that there exists a coherent plan for teaching content within the local district, or even the individual school, is a gravely misleading myth. (1996, p. 26)

In an attempt to alleviate this problem, "standards" have been identified in virtually every major subject area both at the national and state levels.

Standards, particularly at the state level, can help teachers identify the subject-specific content that will be addressed within a grading period. Some state documents provide rather explicit guidance for teachers—for example, specific "benchmarks" at grade levels or grade-level intervals. The following are the grade 6–8 benchmarks for the Florida Department of State (State of Florida, 1996) "sunshine" standard in science entitled "The student understands the basic principles of atomic theory":

> • The student describes and compares the properties of particles and waves.
> • The student knows the general properties of the atom (a massive nucleus of neutral neutrons and positive protons surrounded by a cloud of negative electrons) and accepts that single atoms are not visible.
> • The student knows that radiation, light, and heat are forms of energy used to cook food, treat diseases, and provide energy. (p. 53)

This standard provides an 8th grade teacher in Florida with a great deal of guidance about what information and skill to address in a unit on atomic theory.

Unfortunately, not all state documents provide this level of guidance, as illustrated in a series of studies conducted by the American Federation of Teachers (AFT) (see Gandal, 1995, 1996, 1997; AFT, 1998). When the first AFT report (Gandal, 1995) was published, virtually every state was developing academic standards; however, AFT judged the majority of the standards to be insufficiently clear and specific. AFT's 1998 report, *Making Standards Matter*, noted that the commitment to standards-based reform remains very strong in the states. However, the overall findings indicated that the standards movement at the state level still left much to be accomplished. The major problem continues to be lack of specificity. For example, the 1996 report offered the following example of a mathematics standard from a state document that is too general to provide guidance in the classroom: "Students should be able to represent and solve problems using geometric models" (Gandal, 1996, p. 16). Other studies have observed the same lack of specificity in state standard documents (see Education Week on the Web, 1998; Finn, Petrilli, & Vanourek, 1998). This lack of specificity sometimes causes classroom teachers great difficulty in identifying subject-specific content on which to base their grades. We will consider techniques for dealing with standards that are too general in Chapter 4.

Thinking and Reasoning Skills

A second factor commonly included in academic achievement is thinking and reasoning skills. Teachers perceive the ability to "think about" subject-specific content in complex ways as a necessary condition for mastery of the content. This perceived relationship between academic achievement and thinking and reasoning skills is not unique to classroom teachers. There have been many calls for enhanced thinking and reasoning skills as a formal part of academic content—for example, from the National Science Board Commission on Precollege Education in Mathematics, Science and Technology (1983), the Commis-

sion on the Humanities (1980), the College Board (1983), the National Education Association (Futrell, 1987), and the American Federation of Teachers (1985).

The importance of thinking and reasoning skills as a critical part of academic achievement received its strongest endorsement in September 1989, at the first Education Summit in Charlottesville, Virginia. There, President George Bush and the nation's governors, including then-governor Bill Clinton, agreed on six broad goals for American education, which were published as *The National Education Goals Report: Building a Nation of Learners* (National Education Goals Panel [NEGP], 1991). One of those goals (Goal 3) specifically addressed the enhancement of thinking and reasoning: ". . . and every school in America will ensure that all students learn to use their minds, so they may be prepared for responsible citizenship, further learning, and productive employment in our modern economy" (p. 4).

Although there is general agreement about the importance of teaching thinking and reasoning, there is less agreement on the exact skills that students should learn. In fact, some psychologists maintain that it is illogical to talk about thinking and reasoning in isolation from content. Specifically, in a landmark article Robert Glaser (1984) argued that there are no such constructs as general thinking and reasoning skills that cut across subject-matter boundaries—interdisciplinary thinking and reasoning skills, one might say. Researcher Lauren Resnick supported this position in a popular monograph entitled *Education and Learning to Think* (1987). In contrast, some educators such as Beyer (1988), de Bono (1985), Marzano (1992a, b), and Quellmalz (1987), have developed programs and practices designed to teach and reinforce general thinking and reasoning skills that purportedly apply to all subject areas.

Thus far, the debate has been waged with theory and opinion, with both sides providing equally compelling cases. In an attempt to provide an empirical approach to this issue, researchers at Mid-continent Research for Education and Learning (McREL) turned to national standards documents (see Marzano, Kendall, & Gaddy, 1999; Marzano, 1998b). McREL researchers reasoned that if general thinking and reasoning skills do, in fact, exist, they should be found in the national standards documents. To illustrate, if the standards documents in mathematics, science, and history all mention as important the thinking and reasoning skill of problem solving, then one might conclude that problem solving is a general thinking and reasoning skill that cuts across these subject areas. The national standards documents, then, represent a source from which general thinking and reasoning skills can be gleaned—if they in fact exist.

To study thinking and reasoning in the national documents, McREL researchers focused their attention on the documents listed in Figure 3.2. We analyzed all the documents for thinking and reasoning skills that were stated explicitly and implicitly. In all, six categories of general thinking and reasoning skills were mentioned in a majority of the subject areas. They are listed in Figure 3.3.

In the first column, the 12 subject areas are in rank order by the percentage of total references to thinking and reasoning attributed to each subject area. Some interesting inferences can be made from the data by analyzing the percentages of references for each of the six thinking and reasoning skill areas within specific subjects. For example, science places major emphasis on experi-

mental inquiry because 32.3 percent of its references to thinking and reasoning were specific to this one skill area. Additionally, science places heavy emphasis on the uses of logic, and some emphasis on problem solving and identifying similarities, differences, and patterns. It places relatively minor emphasis on decision making.

I believe these six general thinking and reasoning skills represent the first list ever devised empirically by analyzing national standards documents and, by virtue of the origin of those standards documents, the first list of "consensus" thinking and reasoning skills across the subject areas. Working with teachers, McREL researchers (see Marzano, Mayeski, & Dean, 1999) have found it useful to organize the list in a specific way and to break out some of the thinking and reasoning skills into subcomponents (see Figure 3.4, p. 36).

Figure 3.4 lists 10 thinking and reasoning skills because 2 of the skills have been further specified. Additionally, the 10 skills are organized into 2 broad categories: general information processing and knowledge utilization. It is important to note that there are many lists of thinking and reasoning skills. In fact, some schools and districts have developed their own lists. The point here is that thinking and reasoning skills—whichever list is used—should be thought of as content that is an explicit factor included in grading under the general heading of academic achievement.

General Communication Skills

General communication skills represent the final category of content considered a component of academic achievement. Again, this becomes apparent when one examines the various national- and state-level standards documents. For example,

FIGURE 3.2
Standards Documents Used in McREL Study of Thinking and Reasoning Skills

1. Science:
   - *Benchmarks for Science Literacy* (American Association for the Advancement of Science, 1993)
   - *National Science Education Standards* (National Research Council, 1996)

2. Mathematics:
   - *Curriculum and Evaluation Standards for School Mathematics* (National Council of Teachers of Mathematics, 1989)

3. Social Studies:
   - *Expectations of Excellence: Curriculum Standards for Social Studies* (National Council for the Social Studies, 1994)

4. Geography:
   - *Geography for Life: National Geography Standards* (Geography Education Standards Project, 1994)

5. History:
   - *National Standards for History: Basic Edition* (National Center for History in the Schools, 1996)

6. Civics:
   - *National Standards for Civics and Government* (Center for Civic Education, 1994)

7. Physical Education:
   - *Moving into the Future, National Standards for Physical Education: A Guide to Content and Assessment* (National Association for Sport and Physical Education, 1995)

8. Health:
   - *National Health Education Standards: Achieving Health Literacy* (Joint Committee on National Health Education Standards, 1995)

9. The Arts:
   - *National Standards for Arts Education: What Every Young American Should Know and Be Able to Do in the Arts* (Consortium of National Arts Education Associations, 1994)

10. Foreign Language:
    - *Standards for Foreign Language Learning: Preparing for the 21st Century* (National Standards in Foreign Language Education Project, 1996)

11. The English Language Arts:
    - *Standards in Practice: Grades K–2* (Crafton, 1996)
    - *Standards in Practice: Grades 3–5* (Sierra-Perry, 1996)
    - *Standards in Practice: Grades 6–8* (Wilhelm, 1996)
    - *Standards in Practice: Grades 9–12* (Smagorinski, 1996)

12. The World of Work:
    - *What Work Requires of Schools: A SCANS Report for America 2000* (The Secretary's Commission on Achieving Necessary Skills, 1991)
    - *Workplace Basics: The Essential Skills Employers Want* (Carnevale, Gainer & Meltzer, 1990)

FIGURE 3.3
Percentage of Citations of Various Thinking and Reasoning Skills by Subject Matter

Subject Area	Percent of Total References*	Identifying Similarities, Dissimilarities, & Patterns	Problem Solving	Investigation	Decision Making	Experimental Inquiry	Logic
Science	(27.2%)	8.3%	11.5%	22.9%	3.1%	32.3%	21.8%
History	(13.0%)	32.6%	26.1%	15.2%	15.2%	8.7%	2.2%
Mathematics	(11.3%)	17.5%	50.0%	7.5%	0.0%	20.0%	5.0%
Social Studies	(9.1%)	28.1%	6.3%	28.1%	28.1%	3.1%	6.3%
The Arts	(8.2%)	46.4%	32.1%	7.1%	14.3%	0.0%	0.0%
Civics	(7.4%)	23.1%	38.5%	7.7%	30.8%	0.0%	0.0%
Work	(6.8%)	12.5%	54.2%	20.8%	0.0%	4.2%	8.3%
Foreign Language	(4.0%)	92.9%	0.0%	7.1%	0.0%	0.0%	0.0%
Geography	(3.7%)	30.8%	7.7%	7.7%	30.8%	23.1%	0.0%
Health	(3.7%)	46.2%	15.4%	7.7%	30.8%	0.0%	0.0%
Physical Education	(3.1%)	45.5%	18.2%	0.0%	36.4%	0.0%	0.0%
Language Arts	(2.8%)	50.0%	0.0%	0.0%	10.0%	20.0%	20.0%

*Percentages in this column are across all subject areas. Percentages in each row are for specific content areas only. Thus, the references in science accounted for 27.2% of references across all documents analyzed. Within the subject area of science, 32.3% of thinking skill references were to experimental inquiry.

the National Council of Teachers of Mathematics (NCTM, 1989) identifies communication as one of the 13 general standards for mathematics. The National Science Education standards identify the ability to communicate as a basic skill underlying the content standards. The National Health Education standards (Joint Committee on National Health Education Standards, 1995) note that developing students into "Effective Communicators" (p. 7) underlies all the content standards. Finally, the National Geography standards *Geography for Life* (Geography Education Standards Project, 1994) notes that underlying the attainment of geography information and skill, students should be able "to communicate clearly and effectively" (p. 44).

An analysis of the national standards documents indicates that all subject areas appear to value these three skills:

1. Ability to communicate ideas in written form.

2. Ability to communicate ideas in oral form.

3. Ability to communicate in one or more mediums other than writing or speaking.

FIGURE 3.4
Thinking and Reasoning Skills for Classroom Use Identified by the McREL Study

General Information Processing Skills

Identifying similarities, dissimilarities, and patterns
1. Comparing and contrasting
2. Analyzing relationships
3. Classifying

Logic
4. Argumentation
5. Making inductions
6. Making deductions

Knowledge Utilization Skills

7. Experimental inquiry
8. Investigation
9. Problem Solving
10. Decision Making

The first two categories of communication skills are fairly obvious: the ability to present ideas in written and oral form has been a staple of American education for well over a century. The ability to communicate in media forms other than writing and speaking (such as video presentations and multimedia presentations that employ art or music or both) covers a range of skills, some of which are relatively new products of our technological age.

No matter what medium is used for communication, the following skills are critical—they cut across all forms of communication:

1. Presenting ideas clearly.

2. Altering communications for different audiences.

3. Altering communications for different purposes.

The relationship between these three skills and the three previously mentioned is depicted in Figure 3.5.

Writing, speaking, and communicating in other mediums all involve the skills of presenting ideas clearly and altering presentations for different audiences and for different purposes. Presenting ideas clearly involves having a clear main idea or theme with supporting detail. Another skill that applies to all forms of communication is the ability to communicate with diverse audiences. As students mature, they increase the types of audiences with whom they can effectively communicate. According to current theory in rhetoric (see Durst & Newell, 1989), effectively communicat-

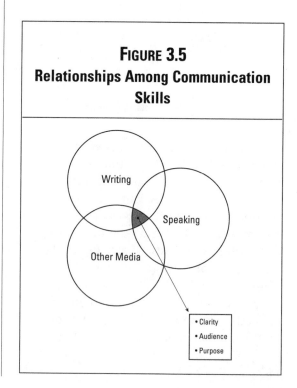

FIGURE 3.5
Relationships Among Communication Skills

ing with any given audience demands a sensitivity to the level of knowledge and understanding of that audience. The third skill is the ability to communicate for a variety of purposes. Researchers have shown that people who have the ability to write for specific purposes have some knowledge of specific rhetorical conventions that are appropriate for some purposes but not others (see Durst & Newell, 1989).

What About the Nonachievement Factors?

In an ideal grading system, effort, behavior, and attendance would not be included with academic achievement in an overall grade. Indeed, research by Cross and Frary (1999) indicates that when asked, 81 percent of teachers and 70 percent of students agreed with or tended to agree with this assertion. Yet, contradictorily, in the same study 39 percent of teachers admitted including effort and behavior in grades. In explaining this apparent contradiction, Brookhart (1994) notes that "present recommendations for grading do not take into account the teacher's need to manage classrooms and motivate students" (p. 299). Teachers perceive the three "nonachievement" factors of effort, behavior, and attendance as important to classroom control and, consequently, often include them in their grading policies.

In Chapter 7, we will look at grading schemes that separate achievement factors from nonachievement factors. In this chapter and those leading to Chapter 7, however, the discussion will assume that a teacher wishes to include these elements in an overall grade. We will first consider the validity of effort, behavior, and attendance as factors on which students should receive feedback.

The Validity of Nonachievement Factors

Is there a valid basis for providing students with feedback on the three nonachievement factors? The answer is an unqualified yes, if one considers reports from the world of work. To illustrate, consider the 1991 report by the Secretary's Commission on Achieving Necessary Skills (SCANS) entitled *What Work Requires of Schools: A SCANS Report for America 2000*. The commission spent 12 months "talking to business owners, to public employees, to the people who manage employees daily, to union officials, and to workers on the line and at their desks. We have talked to them in their stores, shops, government offices, and manufacturing facilities" (p. v). The list of skills that this group identified as "necessary" was heavily weighted in favor of "life skills," which included effort, behavior, and attendance.

A complementary work to the SCANS report, *Workplace Basics: The Essential Skills Employers Want* (Carnevale, Gainer, & Meltzer, 1990), was sponsored by the American Society for Training and Development (ASTD). Representing the opinions of "approximately 50,000 practitioners, managers, administrators, educators, and researchers in the field of human resource development" (p. xiii), the report identifies skills such as personal responsibility, working with others, and self-efficacy as essential for workplace success.

Parents have also articulated the importance of these skills. The polling firm Public Agenda surveyed a representative sample of parents about what should be taught in the schools. Their report, *First Things First: What Americans Expect From Public Schools* (Farkas, Friedman, Boese, & Shaw, 1994), noted that 88 percent of those surveyed said that schools should teach and reinforce work-related competencies such as punctuality, dependability, and self-discipline. In a more generalized poll of U.S. adults conducted by the Gallup Corporation under direction from McREL, the category of "life skills," such as self-regulation and working well in groups, was rated higher than 13 other subject areas (i.e., mathematics, science, history, language arts, physical education, and so on) in terms of those competencies students should "definitely" be required to master before high school graduation (see Marzano, Kendall, & Gaddy, 1999; Marzano, Kendall, & Cicchinelli, 1998).

Defining the Nonachievement Factors

In my work with teachers across the country, three nonachievement factors—effort, behavior, and attendance—seem to strike a chord. They intuitively sense that providing feedback on these factors gets at something very important. Yet, in talking with them, I have discovered that educators define the factors somewhat differently. I have found it useful to subdivide them in this way:

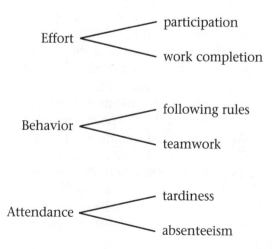

1. Effort

Classroom teachers perceive effort in one of two ways:

• *Participation* is the extent to which a student responds in class and is generally engaged in the activities at hand.

• *Work completion* is the extent to which a student meets expectations about the tasks presented as part of the curriculum. For example, the student turns in assignments in a timely fashion, adhering to the conventions that have been set for those assignments (e.g., typed or written neatly, format considerations met, and so on).

2. Behavior

Behavior is defined in two ways:

• *Following rules* is the extent to which students adhere to the implicit and explicit rules of conduct. This skill manifests as following the letter and intent of school and classroom rules, as well as following the conventions of courteous behavior that may not be stated explicitly in school or classroom rules.

• *Teamwork* is the extent to which students actively participate in group goals. It should be noted that this skill area does not include conduct within a group, because those behaviors are commonly addressed in school or classroom rules. Teamwork manifests as students actively work toward goals defined by a group as opposed to engaging only in their own goals.

3. Attendance

Attendance is divided into two areas:

• *Absenteeism* is the extent to which a student is absent from class.

- *Tardiness* is the extent to which a student comes late to class.

We will see in the next two chapters that the nonachievement factors can be assessed quite accurately and feedback provided to students in a systematic way.

Conclusion

This chapter has made a case for academic achievement as the primary factor to include in grades. Academic achievement is defined as competence in: (1) the specific subject-matter content, (2) thinking and reasoning skills, and (3) general communication skills. Although these should be the primary factors on which grades are based, it is appropriate to provide feedback to students on their effort, behavior, and attendance. Ideally, this feedback should be kept separate from that provided on academic achievement.

4 Keeping Track of Achievement

Academic achievement should be the primary factor in grades. In Chapter 3, however, we saw that the construct of academic achievement is not a simple one. Achievement can include subject-specific content, thinking and reasoning skills, as well as general communication skills. Additionally, teachers may include nonachievement factors in their grading schemes such as effort, behavior, and attendance. To provide effective feedback to students, teachers must keep track of those factors they wish to include in grades. Doing so requires a major shift in the way records are kept.

This chapter and the next present techniques for keeping track of multiple achievement and nonachievement factors. To understand the full impact of these new record-keeping methods, we must first consider how teachers currently keep records. We addressed this topic briefly in Chapter 1. Here we consider current classroom record-keeping practices in some depth.

Classroom Record-Keeping Today

Assume that a teacher has given the following six assignments, quizzes, and tests during a nine-week grading period, each worth a specific number of points. The points assigned to each assessment represent their relative importance. The more important the assessment, the more points it is allocated. For example, the teacher has given the fourth and sixth assessments the highest weights of 40 points each, and the third and fifth assessments the lowest weights of 10 points each.

1. Quiz on September 7:   20 points
2. Homework on September 13:   30 points
3. Homework on September 27:   10 points
4. Performance task on October 2: 40 points
5. Quiz on October 25:   10 points
6. Exam on November 2:   40 points

FIGURE 4.1
Four Students' Scores on Six Assessments

Students	Assessments					
	1	2	3	4	5	6
Todd	19	28	9	38	9	38
Carmen	14	19	9	31	6	35
Jena	19	21	4	20	5	18
Stephanie	17	24	8	33	8	35

(Note: Although a teacher would certainly use more than six assessments during nine weeks, I am limiting the number for ease of illustration and discussion.)

Also, assume that four students in the class received the scores depicted in Figure 4.1 on the six assessments. The fact that each assessment is allotted a specific number of points makes it relatively easy for a teacher to compute a grade. For each student, the teacher simply adds up the points for the various assessments and then divides the total number of earned points by the total number of possible points. These proportions are then turned into percentages by multiplying by 100 (see Figure 4.2).

The percentage scores for each student are then translated into a letter grade using a conversion scale like this one:

93%–100%   = A
85%–92%   = B

FIGURE 4.2
Conversion of Students' Points to Percentages for Six Assessments

Students	1 20 pts.	2 30 pts.	3 10 pts.	4 40 pts.	5 10 pts.	6 40 pts.	Total Points (150 possible)	Total Points Divided by Total Possible Points	Percentage
Todd	19	28	9	38	9	38	141	.94	94%
Carmen	14	19	9	31	6	35	114	.76	76%
Jena	19	21	4	20	5	18	87	.58	58%
Stephanie	17	24	8	33	8	35	125	.83	83%

75%–84%   = C
65%–74%   = D
64% or below = F

Using this scheme, Todd would receive an *A*, Carmen and Stephanie would receive *C*'s, and Jena would receive an *F*.

A variation on this same scheme is to record percentage scores for each assessment and then weight the percentage scores in accordance with the relative importance of each assessment. To illustrate, consider Carmen's six scores: 14, 19, 9, 31, 6, and 35. When computed as percentages, these scores are 70%, 63%, 90%, 78%, 60%, and 88% respectively. The teacher would multiply each percentage score by the weight associated with that assessment. If the first assessment was given a weight of 2, then Carmen's weighted score for that assessment would be 140 (2 × 70). At the end of the grading period, weighted scores are added up and the sum divided by the total weights to obtain an average score that is then translated into an overall grade.

The weighted percentage method is fundamentally identical to the point method. The only difference is the time at which scores on assessments are translated to percentages. With the point method, the translation to percentage scores is done at the end of the grading period; with the percentage method, it is done immediately after each assessment. In the remainder of this text, I will use the terms *point method* and *percentage method* interchangeably.

Given the intuitive appeal of the point or percentage method, one might legitimately ask what is wrong with it. As we shall see, there is much to warrant scepticism about this approach.

The Problem with Points

Before detailing the many problems with the point method, it is only fair to discuss the one situation in which it has some validity. Specifically, the point method makes sense if a teacher addresses only one topic within a grading period. To illustrate, assume that Figure 4.3 represents four assessments on the same topic and that each assessment measures differing amounts of the knowledge and skill within that topic. As depicted, the first assessment measures twice as much of the information and skill

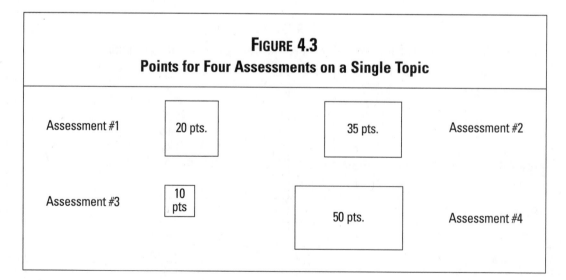

FIGURE 4.3
Points for Four Assessments on a Single Topic

Assessment #1   20 pts.   35 pts.   Assessment #2

Assessment #3   10 pts   50 pts.   Assessment #4

in the topic as the third. Therefore, it receives twice the number of points. The fourth assessment measures five times as much of the information and skill in the topic as does the third assessment and, consequently, receives five times the points. Given that all four assessments differ only in the amount of information and skill they address, adding up the points a student accumulates should provide a fairly accurate picture of a student's achievement in that topic. For example, assume that a student obtained the following scores on the four assessments depicted in Figure 4.3:

Assessment #1:   13/20
Assessment #2:   19/35
Assessment #3:   6/10
Assessment #4:   41/50
Total: 79/115 = 68.7%

Seventy-nine out of one hundred and fifteen points, or 68.7 percent, is probably a

fair representation of the student's achievement in the topic.

The point or percentage method, then, does make sense assuming that all assessments address a single topic. However, rarely is a single topic addressed within a grading period. More often than not, multiple topics are addressed not just during a grading period, but within a single assessment. To illustrate, Figure 4.4 depicts a pattern in which four topics are distributed across eight assessments, which include four homework assignments, two quizzes, one comprehensive exam, and one performance task. Each assessment addresses a somewhat different combination of topics. Additionally, the total for each assessment is a combination of points for the topics addressed within the assessment. For example, the 40 points assigned to the performance task is a composite of 10 points on topic #1, 10 points on topic #2, and 20 points on topic #3. Therefore, a student's

FIGURE 4.4
Multiple Topics Distributed Across Various Assessments

Assessment	Topic #1	Topic #2	Topic #3	Topic #4
Homework #1 (10 points)	5 points		5 points	
Homework #2 (10 points)	5 points	5 points		
Quiz #1 (15 points)	5 points	5 points	5 points	
Homework #3 (15 points)	5 points			10 points
Quiz #2 (20 points)	5 points	5 points		10 points
Performance Task (40 points)	10 points	10 points	20 points	
Homework #4 (10 points)			5 points	5 points
Final Exam (100 points)	20 points	20 points	20 points	40 points
Total: 220 points	55 points	45 points	55 points	65 points

score—total points—on any assessment is a combination of the scores he or she received on different topics.

Uneven patterns in topic coverage across assessments such as this illustrate how misleading the point or percentage method can be in summarizing student achievement. In fact, adding up points across quizzes, homework, and so forth can give a very inaccurate picture of student achievement. Consider two students who received the same total points for a grading period: 150 out of a possible 220 for a percentage score of 68 percent. Figure 4.5 shows the scores the students received on the various topics addressed in each assessment.

Although both students acquired the same number of total points, they performed quite differently on the four topics addressed. For example, Student #1 scored 51 out of 55 points (or 93%) for topic #1, but Student #2 scored only 24 out of 55 points (or 44%) on topic #1. Conversely, Student #1 scored 31 of 55 points (or 56%) on topic #3, whereas Student #2 obtained 42 of 55 points (or 76%) on topic #3. The very different profiles of the two students on the four topics is graphically illustrated in Figure 4.6.

Student #1 has performed relatively well on topics 1 and 2 and not so well on topics 3 and 4. Student #2 has performed quite poorly on topic #1, and marginally well on topics 2, 3, and 4. If grades were based only on their achievement in a *single topic,* both students would have received different grades depending on the topic that was considered (see Figure 4.7, p. 47).

Clearly, these two students have very different achievement profiles in the four topics addressed during the grading period. Yet, when we add up their scores on the various homework assignments, quizzes, and so forth, they have the same final score and, consequently, the same final grade. In short, not considering the differing levels of achievement across the various topics addressed in a grading period plays havoc with a teacher's ability to provide accurate feedback to students.

Where Did the Point Method Come From?

Given how entrenched we are in the point or percentage method of assigning scores to students, it is useful to consider its history. How did it become so popular? Measurement expert Darrell Bock (1997) traces its origin to World War I. He notes that faced with the problem of quickly and efficiently determining the competencies of hundreds of thousands of recruits, the U.S. Army developed the Alpha Test. Its purpose was to assess the aptitude of new American soldiers in order to place them in work roles that were most appropriate to their abilities. Given the need for ease of scoring due to the large number of soldiers who would take the test, the Army Alpha Test relied primarily on multiple-choice items that could be scored as correct or incorrect: correct items received one point; incorrect items received no points. Generally speaking, the test was considered highly successful. Tens of thousands of recruits were assessed quickly and efficiently and their scores used to place them in specific jobs. The success of the Army's easily scored test soon made the multiple-choice item the preferred tool in a wide variety of assessment situations.

The multiple-choice format received its strongest endorsement in education when in the early 1940s the College Entrance Examination Board (CEEB) commissioned psychologist Carl Bingham to develop the Scholastic Aptitude Test, which was in-

FIGURE 4.5 — Score Patterns for Two Students Who Received the Same Total Points for a Grading Period					
Student #1					
Assessment	Total Scores for Student	Student's Scores on Topic #1	Student's Scores on Topic #2	Student's Scores on Topic #3	Student's Scores on Topic #4
Homework #1	7/10	3 out of 5		4 out of 5	
Homework #2	8/10	5 out of 5	3 out of 5		
Quiz #1	7/15	4 out of 5	2 out of 5	1 out of 5	
Homework #3	8/15	5 out of 5			3 out of 10
Quiz #2	17/20	5 out of 5	5 out of 5		7 out of 10
Performance Task	28/40	10 out of 10	8 out of 10	10 out of 20	
Homework #4	6/10			5 out of 5	1 out of 5
Final Exam	69/100	19 out of 20	18 out of 20	11 out of 20	21 out of 40
	150/220 (68%)	51/55 (93%)	36/45 (80%)	31/55 (56%)	32/65 (49%)
Student #2					
Homework #1	6/10	1 out of 5		5 out of 5	
Homework #2	7/10	2 out of 5	5 out of 5		
Quiz #1	9/15	2 out of 5	4 out of 5	3 out of 5	
Homework #3	9/15	3 out of 5			6 out of 10
Quiz #2	14/20	1 out of 5	4 out of 5		9 out of 10
Performance Task	30/40	3 out of 10	9 out of 10	18 out of 20	
Homework #4	4/10			1 out of 5	3 out of 5
Final Exam	71/100	12 out of 20	11 out of 20	15 out of 20	33 out of 40
	150/220 (68%)	24/55 (44%)	33/45 (73%)	42/55 (76%)	51/65 (78%)

tended to predict success in college. The test was designed to address general aptitude as opposed to knowledge of specific subject matter, which had been the focus of previous CEEB tests. Because of the ease with which multiple-choice items could be scored, the written essay portion of the college entrance examination was dropped by 1942. Prior to that date, the essay portion of the SAT was the most heavily weighted component. By 1947, the multiple-choice format was a permanent fixture in the SAT.

FIGURE 4.6
Profiles of Two Students' Percentage Scores on Four Topics

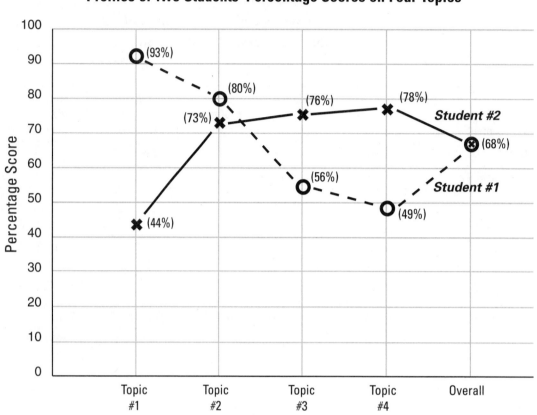

This was in no small part due to the development of the mechanical mark-sense answer sheets, as Bock explains:

> Because the early equipment could do no more than count the number of pencil marks in the correct boxes of the item alternatives, the number-correct score became by default the source datum for theoretical work in educational measurement. It became the main focus of test theory. (1997, p. 23)

The perceived utility of the multiple-choice format soon spilled over to any item that could be scored as correct or incorrect: 1 or 0. This included item formats such as true/false, matching, and fill-in-the-blank. In fact, theoretical constructs in measurement theory such as reliability, validity, and the extent to which an item differentiates between students who do well on a test versus those who do poorly (technically referred to as item discrimination) were developed under the assumption that items were scored as correct or incorrect (see Lord & Novick, 1968; Gulliksen, 1950; Magnussen, 1966).

Quite naturally, courses and textbooks that were designed to help teachers construct and interpret classroom assessments adopted the correct/incorrect heuristic for scoring items on tests. Additionally, the

FIGURE 4.7
Topic Grades for Two Students Based Only on Their Achievement in Each Topic

Topic on Which Grade Is Based	Student #1's Grades	Student #2's Grades
1	A	F
2	C	D
3	F	C
4	F	C

ratio of the total number of correct responses over the total possible correct responses translated to a percentage score was adopted as an indication of students' general achievement in the domain being assessed. From there, it wasn't much of a step to assign points to assessments that could not be scored as correct or incorrect, such as essay items, oral presentations, and the like. Without realizing it, educators were soon entrenched in the point or percentage method. To this date, it has rarely been questioned.

This book assumes that the point or percentage method is inadequate to the task of tracking achievement on multiple topics in a rigorous fashion. What, then, is a classroom teacher to do? The answer is fairly straightforward and basic. To effectively keep track of achievement when multiple topics are addressed within a grading period requires fundamental changes in the way teachers keep records, design and score tests, then summarize those scores at the end of a grading period. We will begin by discussing a new technique for keeping a grade book.

From Columns to Rows and Points to Rubrics

The changes required to effectively address multiple topics within a grading period are simple, but profound. These changes are depicted in Figure 4.8. Here the columns of the grade book do not represent the various quizzes, homework assignments, tests, and performance tasks assigned throughout the grading period, as they do in a regular grade book (compare Figure 4.8 to Figure 4.2). Rather, the columns represent the various topics addressed during the grading period: precipitation, ocean currents, measurement of temperature, reading tables, and estimation. It is the rows of the grade book that represent the assessments assigned throughout the grading period. For example, as indicated in the assessment key at the top of the page, the first row (i.e., row A) for each student represents quiz #1 given on September 10; the next row for each student represents the homework assignment given on September 10, and so on.

One major difference, then, between this grade book and the traditional one is the use of rows to represent assessments and columns to represent categories of knowledge and skill. Of course, this convention means that the "topics-focused" grade book will be much larger. In fact, if a teacher assigns a large number of assessments during a grading period, a full page might be required for each student. If the grade book depicted in Figure 4.8 is kept on a computer, the problems of space are cleared up immediately. In the next chapter we will consider how specific computer programs make implementing this system easy and efficient. For now, however, let's assume that a teacher is using a grade book that requires entries by hand. Appendix B

FIGURE 4.8
A Topics-Based Grade Book

Assessment Key:		
A. Quiz: Sept. 10	F. Unit Test #1: Sept. 22	K. Quiz: Oct. 8
B. Homework: Sept. 10	G. Performance Task: Sept. 24	L. Homework: Oct. 11
C. Homework: Sept. 15	H. Homework: Sept. 29	M. Homework: Oct. 13
D. Homework: Sept. 17	I. Quiz: Oct. 1	N. Quiz: Oct. 15
E. Quiz: Sept. 20	J. Homework: Oct. 6	O. Unit Test-Performance Task: Oct. 6

Students/Assessments		Topics				
		Precipitation	Ocean Currents	Measurement of Temperature	Reading Tables	Estimation
Bill	A	1.5		1.0		2.0
	B	2.0			1.5	
	C	1.5				2.0
	D	2.0				
	E	1.5		1.5		2.0
	F	2.0		1.5	1.5	
	G	2.5		1.5	1.5	2.0
	H		2.0			
	I		2.0			
	J			2.0	1.5	
	K		2.0		2.0	
	L		2.0			
	M		2.5			
	N		2.5			
	O	2.5	2.5	2.0	2.0	
Final Topic Score		2.25	2.5	1.5	1.75	2.0
Marv	A	3.0		4.0		3.0
	B	4.0			3.5	
	C	3.5				3.5
	D	4.0				
	E	4.0		4.0		3.5
	F	3.5		3.5	3.5	
	G	3.5		3.5	4.0	3.5
	H		4.0			
	I		4.0			
	J			3.5	4.0	
	K		3.5		4.0	
	L		3.5			
	M		4.0			
	N		3.5			
	O	3.5	4.0	4.0	4.0	
Final Topic Score		3.75	3.75	3.75	4.0	3.5

Note: Final topic scores are not necessarily averages of column scores.

contains a sample grade book page which may be duplicated by teachers and adapted to suit their needs (p. 124).

Even when a full page is used for each student, teachers who have used this system report the increased number of pages does not require a great increase in the time and energy needed to maintain a grade. We will consider in depth the issue of how much time this system takes in Chapter 5.

Assigning Multiple Scores Using Rubrics

Another major difference between a topic-based grade book and the traditional grade book is that assessments are scored on more than one topic using a scoring system other than tallying up points. To illustrate, consider the homework on September 10 (row B for each student)—it addressed topic 1 (precipitation) and topic 4 (reading tables). Therefore, each student received two scores on that quiz—one for topic #1 and one for topic #4. Also note that all the scores in Figure 4.8 range from 0 to 4 because four-point rubrics have been used.

By now, most teachers are quite familiar with the concept of a rubric. Although there are different perspectives on the nature and function of rubrics (for discussion, see Wiggins, 1993a, 1993b; Stiggins, 1994, 1997; Marzano, Pickering, & McTighe, 1993), most advocates agree on at least one basic feature—namely that rubrics should describe levels of performance or understanding for a particular topic. For example, assume that a teacher whose grade book is depicted in Figure 4.8 wished to design a rubric for the topic of precipitation. The rubric the teacher might use is depicted in the left column of Figure 4.9.

Notice that in this rubric the teacher has identified the key feature of the topic—the relationship between temperature and precipitation—and the levels of understanding important to this feature. Designing a rubric like this is not as difficult as it might appear because rubrics tend to follow general patterns. Thus, using generic rubrics, teachers can design topic-specific rubrics like the one just stated. To illustrate, the right column of Figure 4.9 contains the generic rubric used to create the topic-specific rubric about precipitation.

The logic underlying the generic rubric is fairly straightforward. At level 4, students understand the important information accurately and in detail. At level 3, they understand the important information accurately but not in detail. At level 2, students have an incomplete understanding and/or have some misconceptions about the important information; however, they still know enough to have a basic understanding of the topic. At level 1, students have so many misconceptions or their knowledge is so incomplete that they cannot be said to possess an understanding of the topic. Finally, a score of 0 indicates that the student provided little or no information with which to make a judgment. For example, the student did not answer the questions designed to assess knowledge of the topic of precipitation.

Armed with the simple generic rubric depicted in the right column of Figure 4.9, teachers can easily design rubrics for the specific topics in their courses. It is important to note that the generic rubric is for "information-based topics." Topics generally come in two basic types: (1) information-based, or (2) process- or skill-based. As the name indicates, information-based topics are composed of concepts, principles, generalizations, and details. The topic of

---

FIGURE 4.9
Topic-Specific and Generic Rubric for Information-Based Topics

Topic-Specific Rubric for Precipitation	Generic Rubric for Information-Based Topics
4 The student has a complete and detailed understanding of the information important to the topic of precipitation (particularly the relationship between temperature and precipitation).	4 The student has a complete and detailed understanding of the information important to the topic.
3 The student has a complete but not detailed understanding of the information important to the topic of precipitation (particularly the relationship between temperature and precipitation). There are no misconceptions in the student's knowledge.	3 The student has a complete understanding of the information important to the topic but not in great detail.
2 The student has an incomplete understanding of the information important to the topic of precipitation (particularly the relationship between temperature and precipitation) or has some misconceptions about the information. However, the student still has a basic understanding of the topic.	2 The student has an incomplete understanding of the topic and/or misconceptions about some of the information. However, the student maintains a basic understanding of the topic.
1 The student's understanding of the topic of precipitation (particularly the relationship between temperature and precipitation) is so incomplete and/or there are so many misconceptions that the student does not possess even a basic understanding of the topic.	1 The student's understanding of the topic is so incomplete or has so many misconceptions that the student cannot be said to understand the topic.
0 No judgment can be made about the student's understanding of this topic.	0 No judgment can be made about the student's understanding of the topic.

precipitation is clearly information-based. Process- or skill-based topics are focused on a specific process or skill. A generic rubric that is useful for this type of topic is shown on the right side of Figure 4.10.

The logic behind this rubric is also fairly straightforward. At level 4, students can perform the skill or process and understand how it works. At level 3, students can perform the skill or process without error but cannot describe how it works. At level 2, students make errors, some significant, when performing the skill or process but still accomplish at least a rough approxima-

FIGURE 4.10
Topic-Specific and Generic Rubric for Process- or Skill-Based Topics

Topic-Specific Rubric for Reading Tables	Generic Rubric for Processes or Skills
4 The student can interpret tables without making significant errors. Additionally, the student performs the process with fluency and understands key features of tables.	4 The student can perform the skill or process important to the topic with no significant errors and with fluency. Additionally, the student understands the key features of the skill or process.
3 The student interprets tables without making significant errors.	3 The student can perform the skill or process important to the topic without making significant errors.
2 The student makes some significant errors when interpreting the tables but still accomplishes a basic approximation of the process.	2 The student makes some significant errors when performing the skill or process important to the topic but still accomplishes a rough approximation of the skill or process.
1 The student makes so many errors when interpreting tables that he or she is not capable of reading tables.	1 The student makes so many errors in performing the skill or process important to the topic that he or she cannot actually perform the skill or process.
0 No judgment can be made about the student's ability to interpret tables.	0 No judgment can be made about the student's ability to perform the skill or process.

tion of it. At level 1, students make so many errors that the skill or process breaks down. A score of 0 means that students' response on an assessment does not provide the teacher with enough information to make a judgment.

To illustrate how this generic rubric can be used, consider the topic "reading tables" found in column 4 of the grade book in Figure 4.8. The act of reading tables is clearly process oriented. The left side of Figure 4.10 depicts the topic-specific rubric that might be used to assess students' abil-

ity to read tables. The topic-specific rubric is reported on the left, and the generic rubric on which this topic-specific rubric is based is on the right for comparative purposes.

One last point about assigning multiple scores using rubrics: Topics must be at an appropriate level of generality or, more accurately, an appropriate level of specificity. In the years spent developing this system, I have concluded that state-level standards documents are far too general to be used for precise feedback to students. To illustrate, consider Figure 4.11, which articu-

---

FIGURE 4.11
Sample High School Benchmarks for Standard on Data Analysis and Statistics

- Selects and uses the best method of representing and describing a set of data (e.g., scatter plot, line graph, two-way table).

- Understands measures of central tendency and variability (e.g., standard deviation, range, quartile deviation) and their applications to specific situations.

- Understands the concept of correlation (e.g., the difference between a "true" correlation and a "believable" correlation; when two variables are correlated).

- Understands different methods of curve-fitting (e.g., median-fit line, regression line) and various applications (e.g., making predictions) of these methods.

- Understands how outliers may affect various representations of data (e.g., a regression line might be strongly influenced by a few aberrant points, whereas the scatter plot for the same data might suggest that the aberrant points represent mistakes).

- Understands how the reader's bias, measurement error, and display distortion can affect the interpretation of data.

- Understands sampling distributions, the central limit theorem, and confidence intervals.

- Understands how concepts of representativeness, randomness, and bias in sampling can affect experimental outcomes and statistical interpretations.

- Understands that making an inference about a population from a sample always involves uncertainty and the role of statistics is to estimate the size of that uncertainty.

---

lates recommended high school content within a standard entitled "data analysis and statistics."

The sample mathematics standard and its related content in Figure 4.11 are not taken from a specific state standards document. Rather, they are a composite representation extracted from a number of state and national science documents (for a discussion, see Kendall and Marzano, 1997). They are, however, indicative of the level of generality and organization found in most state-level documents. The point made by Figure 4.11 is that even though all the content listed (commonly referred to as benchmarks) relates to the general area of data analysis and statistics, benchmarks can be organized into a number of more specific topics. Specifically, the benchmarks in Figure 4.11 quite naturally fall into relatively specific topics that include displaying data graphically, distributions, errors in data display, and correlation and prediction. These topics are at about the right level of specificity for designing classroom-level learning objectives, whereas the overall standard "data analysis and statistics" is too general.

For the classroom teacher, this means that the first step in translating state-level standards into a format useful for classroom instruction is to "unpack" the elements in each standard into more homogeneous categories or topics. These more specific categories can then form the basis for constructing learning objectives that can be effectively assessed using rubrics. As an exercise to this end, I have unpacked the mathematics standards found in a variety of state and national documents (see Marzano, 1999). The topics into which those unpacked benchmarks fall are listed in Figure 4.12. Each of the 52 topics identified is at a level of generality suitable for the design of classroom objectives, whereas the standards are too general to be useful at the classroom level.

A New Way of Designing and Scoring Assessments

Armed with topic-specific rubrics, a teacher is well equipped to score classroom assessments in a way that provides students with highly specific feedback. To illustrate, assume that a teacher has designed the assessment in Figure 4.13 as a quiz to measure student achievement in topics 1 and 4 in Figure 4.8: precipitation and reading tables.

The key to designing assessments that can be scored on multiple topics is to make clear which items measure which topics. In the sample quiz in Figure 4.13, items 1, 2, 3, and 5 are designed to measure students' ability to read a table. Items 4, 6, 7, and 8 are designed to assess students' understanding of the topic of precipitation.

With the rubric-based approach to scoring assessments, the teacher still considers students' accuracy in answering each item on the test; however, the items are not scored independently, as is done when points are assigned to items and then added up. Rather, the teacher considers the

responses to all items that pertain to a given topic as a *set of information* with which to make a judgment about student understanding and skill in that topic. Consider Figure 4.14 (p. 56).

For ease of discussion, the responses of two students—Student A and Student B—have been placed side by side. Because this assessment was designed to measure two topics—precipitation and reading tables—two rubrics are used. Although we discussed these rubrics earlier, they are reproduced in brief in Figure 4.15 (p. 57) for ease of discussion.

Somewhat counterintuitively, reports by teachers who have used the rubric system indicate that it is easier to read each student's paper separately for each topic. More specifically, if a quiz is designed to assess two topics, all student papers are read for the first topic and a rubric score assigned to each paper. All papers are then read a second time, during which a rubric score for the second topic is assigned to each paper.

Another convention that increases the accuracy of scoring is to use interim values on rubrics. This approach was recommended by measurement experts Lee Cronbach, Norman Bradburn, and Daniel Horvitz (1994). They explain that unnecessary error occurs when a judge must label a borderline response either 4.0 or 3.0. Recording 3.5 as the judgment can only render the assigned score more accurate (p. 37).

Given the increased precision it brings to the task of scoring assessments, I wholeheartedly endorse Cronbach, Bradburn, and Horvitz's recommendation. Thus, a four-point rubric actually has seven values. (Note that a score of 0 is reserved for situations where no judgment can be made.)

4.0
3.5 Achievement between a score of 3 and 4.

FIGURE 4.12
Topics Within a Variety of Mathematics Standards Documents

Standards	Topics	Standards	Topics
Problem Solving	1. Problem representations 2. Communication and discussion as a problem-solving strategy 3. Inductive and deductive reasoning within problem solving 4. Strategy generations and use	Geometry	26. Shapes and figures 27. Lines 28. Scale 29. Motion geometry 30. Model construction 31. Pythagorean theorem and right triangle 32. Polar coordinates 33. Vectors
Concept of Numbers	5. Whole numbers/integers 6. Fractions 7. Decimals 8. Mixed numbers 9. Sets 10. Different number system 11. Notation 12. Exponents	Data and Statistics	34. Graphs and data display 35. Sampling 36. Central tendency and dispersion 37. Hypothesis generation and testing 38. Errors in data display 39. Correlation and prediction
Computation	13. Addition/subtraction 14. Multiplication/division 15. Estimation 16. Roots 17. Recurrence relationships 18. Matrices	Probability	40. Chance/likelihood 41. Prediction of events using probability 42. Simulation 43. Mathematical modeling of probability 44. Randomness 45. The normal curve and other distributions
Measurement	19. Length/width/height 20. Time/temperature 21. Perimeter/area/volume/mass/circumference 22. Angle 23. Tools and units of measurement 24. Estimation of measurement 25. Rate/velocity/acceleration	Algebra	46. Patterns 47. Variables 48. Expressions 49. Rectangular coordinates 50. Functions 51. Equality and inequality 52. Basic trigonometry functions

Source: Marzano, R. J. (1999). Building curriculum and assessment around standards. In *The High School Magazine 6* (5), 16. Copyright © 1999 by National Association of Secondary School Principals (NASSP). Reprinted by permission. For more information concerning NASSP services and/or programs, please call 703-860-0200.

FIGURE 4.13
A Quiz on Precipitation and Reading Tables

The table below shows the temperature and precipitation (rain or snow) in five different towns on the same day.

Weather Conditions	Town A	Town B	Town C	Town D	Town E
Low Temperature	13°C	–9°C	22°C	–12°C	10°C
High Temperature	25°C	–3°C	30°C	–4°C	12°C
Precipitation	0 cm	5 cm	2 cm	0 cm	10 cm
Humidity	Low	High	Medium	Low	High

1. Which town had the highest temperature?

2. Which town had the most precipitation?

3. Which town or towns had a combination of high humidity and high precipitation?

4. Which towns are the most likely to be located close to each other?

5. Imagine that the table was turned on its side so that the towns (A, B, C, D, and E) were the rows and the information about temperature, precipitation, and humidity was reported in the columns. Would this make it easier or harder to read the table? Explain your answer.

6. Pick one town that probably received snow and two that probably did not but for different reasons. Explain why you think each of the three towns did or did not receive snow.

7. Explain what might have happened if the low temperature in Town E had dropped to –5°C.

8. Explain the relationship between humidity and precipitation if there is one.

FIGURE 4.14
Responses of Two Students to Quiz on Precipitation and Reading Tables (Figure 4.13)

Student A	Student B
1. Which town had the highest temperature?	
Town C because 22°C and 30°C are the higher temperatures.	Town C.
2. Which town had the most precipitation?	
Town E because 10 cm is more precipitation than any other town had.	Town E.
3. Which town or towns had a combination of high humidity and high precipitation?	
Town E had a great deal of precipitation and high humidity.	Town E and maybe B.
4. Which towns are most likely to be close together? Explain your answer.	
The totals for highest temperature, lowest temperature, and precipitation for town A is 38 and for town E is 32. These are closer than any other towns.	B and D were very close in temperature. Only difference is precipitation.
5. Imagine that the table was turned on its side so that the towns (A, B, C, D, and E) were the rows and the information about temperature, precipitation, and humidity was reported in the columns. Would this make it easier or harder to read the table? Explain your answer.	
It would be easier to read because the information would be clearer to read. The way it is now, it's hard to figure out how the pieces of information fit together.	I look at the columns first so it would be easier to see the information about temperature, precipitation, and humidity
6. Pick one town that probably received snow and two that probably did not but for different reasons. Explain why you think each of the three towns did or did not receive snow.	
Town B probably had snow because the temperature was below freezing and there was precipitation. Town C didn't have snow because it was warm but they had rain. Town D didn't have snow because it was too cold.	B had snow for sure. D didn't—there wasn't any precipitation. C didn't because it wasn't cold enough.
7. Explain what might have happened if the lowest temperature in Town E had dropped to –5°C.	
Town E would have gotten snow because it was cold enough	It would have snowed but melted.
8. Explain the relationship between humidity and precipitation if there is one.	
When there is medium or high humidity there is precipitation	You can't say for sure that there is one. You can have high humidity without any precipitation.

FIGURE 4.15
Topic-Specific Rubrics in Brief

Rubric for Reading Tables	Rubric for Precipitation
4 The student can interpret tables without making errors. Additionally, the student understands key features of tables.	4 The student has a complete and detailed understanding of the information important to the topic.
3 The student interprets tables without making significant errors.	3 The student has a complete understanding of the information important to the topic but not in great detail.
2 The student makes some significant errors when interpreting the tables but still accomplishes a basic approximation of the process.	2 The student has an incomplete understanding of the topic and/or misconceptions about some of the information. However, the student maintains a basic understanding of the topic.
1 The student makes so many errors when interpreting tables that he or she is not capable of reading tables.	1 The student's understanding of the topic is so incomplete or has so many misconceptions that the student cannot be said to understand the topic.
0 No judgment can be made about the student's ability to interpret tables.	0 No judgment can be made about the student's understanding of the topic.

3.0

2.5 Achievement between a score of 2 and 3.

2.0

1.5 Achievement between a score of 1 and 2.

1.0

0 No information to make a judgment scale like those described above.

With this system, teachers make judgments like the following:

The student's response does not warrant a score as high as a 3, but it also does not warrant a score as low as a 2. Therefore, a score of 2.5 is assigned.

To illustrate the use of interim values, we will apply the concept to the responses for Students A and B reported in Figure 4.14. We first consider the items designed to assess students' ability to read tables: 1, 2, 3, and 5. Examining the responses for Student A, we see that he identified appropriate towns in items 1, 2, and 3. On the surface, it might look as if he is reading the table without significant error, which would indicate a rubric score of 3. However, upon closer examination of his responses, we find some errors. For example, in item #1, the student correctly identified town C as that with the highest temperature, but his explanation is that 22°C and 30°C are higher temperatures than others in the table. The student has read the rows for both high temperature and low temperature in answering this question. This action might indicate a lack of understanding about how tables are read. Additionally, in item #3, he has correctly identified Town E as one with high precipitation and high humidity. However, the student did not identify Town B, which also had higher humidity and precipitation than any other town except for E. Finally, an examination of Student A's response to item #5 indicates that he does not have a grasp of the basic design of a table.

When I have asked teachers in workshops to score Student A's responses for items 1, 2, 3, and 5, the vast majority have assigned a score of 2.5. They argue that a score of 2 indicates that "significant errors" are made and a score of 3 indicates that no significant errors are made. The responses of Student A do not warrant a 3 because errors of some consequence were made. However, the responses do not warrant a 2 either because the student has completed more than a rough approximation of the process of reading a table. Therefore, teachers assign a score of 2.5.

We now apply the rubric to Student B's responses. Because Student B has no apparent errors in the responses to items 1, 2, 3, and 5, the student's score is at least a 3. A score of 4 would indicate that the student not only performs the skill accurately, but understands how it works. The student's response to item 5 certainly indicates at least some understanding of how tables are organized and how they work. Notice that the student has described the relationship be-

tween the information in the columns versus the rows and how it affects the ease with which a table can be read. It appears, then, that the student has some insight into the nature of tables and the process of reading them. However, the student does not provide a great deal of information with which to make a judgment. In workshops where I have presented the responses of Student B, most teachers believe that a reasonable judgment is that the student's response rates somewhere between a 3 and a 4 and, therefore, assign a rubric score of 3.5.

To score students on their understanding of the topic precipitation, the appropriate information-based rubric in Figure 4.15 would be applied to the responses to items 4, 6, 7, and 8. The reasoning most teachers in my workshop have applied to the responses of Students A and B is reported in Figure 4.16.

What If I Insist on Adding Up Points?

Given how ingrained the point system is in the culture of classroom assessment, some teachers I have worked with simply cannot forego assigning points to items and then adding them up. These teachers frequently ask if the point or percentage method can be used to keep track of student achievement on specific topics. My begrudging answer is that it can be adapted to keep track of performance on specific topics, but does not provide the flexibility of rubrics. However, in deference to those teachers who wish to score tests using points, we will examine how that method can be adapted to keeping track of specific topics.

If points were used to score this assessment, a certain number of points would be assigned to each of the eight items. A judgment is then made about whether each re-

---

FIGURE 4.16
Teachers' Rationale for Scores Given to Students
on Their Understanding of Precipitation

Student A:

The student exhibits some understanding of the topic, but there are certainly misconceptions as indicated by his misunderstanding of the role of humidity relative to precipitation and his inability to explain that the snow would have melted in town E if the temperature had dropped to –5°. Additionally, the student's response to question 4 indicates some confusion. The student's responses fit well with the description of a level 2 on the rubric.

Student B:

The student's responses to questions 6, 7, and 8 are all correct indicating that her score should be at least a 3. To receive a 4, the student would have to exhibit knowledge in great detail. There is no evidence of this due to the sparseness of the student's response. Therefore, a score of 3 seems reasonable.

---

sponse receives the total possible points, indicating that the answer is totally correct; partial points, indicating that part of the answer is correct; or no points, indicating the answer is totally incorrect.

In workshops, I have given the responses of Students A and B to teachers and asked them to assign the total possible points to each item and then score the response of each student. Figure 4.17 depicts the most common scoring patterns.

When points are used to keep track of topic scores, they are assigned to student responses for each item. However, the overall percentage score for an assessment is not computed. Rather, a percentage score is computed for each topic by adding the total points on the items for that topic and dividing by the total possible points, as shown below:

Reading Tables
Student A: 2/5 =
  .40 × 100 = 40%

Precipitation
Student A: 5/9 =
  .56 × 100 = 56%

Student B: 5/5 =
  1.00 × 100 = 100%

Student B: 8/9 =
  .89 × 100 = 89%

As indicated, percentage scores can be used to keep track of student achievement on specific topics. However, they sometimes provide a slightly different picture of students than does the rubric method, as shown here:

Reading Tables
Student A:
  Percentage Score = 40
  Rubric Score = 2.5

Student B:
  Percentage Score = 100
  Rubric Score = 3.5

Precipitation
Student A:
  Percentage Score = 55
  Rubric Score = 2.0

Student B:
  Percentage Score = 89
  Rubric Score = 3.0

Certainly, the percentage scores and the rubric scores convey the same basic message about student performance in the two topics. Student A did not perform very well on the topic of reading tables or on the topic of precipitation. Student B performed

FIGURE 4.17
Point and Percentage Scores for Two Students

Item	Total Possible Points	Points for Student A	Points for Student B
1	1	0	1
2	1	1	1
3	1	1	1
4	2	0	2
5	2	0	2
6	3	2	2
7	2	2	2
8	2	1	2
Total	14	7	13
Overall Percentage Score		50%	93%

fairly well on the topic of precipitation and extremely well on the topic of reading tables. However, the rubric-based approach seems to provide more detail, particularly at the extremes. To illustrate, consider Student B's score on the topic of reading tables. The percentage score is 100, indicating a perfect response; however, the rubric score is 3.5, indicating room for improvement. As we have seen, there was certainly nothing wrong with Student B's responses to the items designed to measure this topic. Taken as a whole, however, they did not warrant a score of 4.

Why do teachers tend to give Student B a perfect score on the topic of tables when points are used and a score less than perfect when rubrics are used? I believe the main reason is that teachers who use the rubrics are considering the four items de-

signed to measure the topic as a set rather than as individual items. When viewed as a set, the four items provide more information than do the items considered in isolation. To use a well-worn phrase, "The whole is greater than the sum of the parts." The rubric method encourages teachers to consider information within and across items. The point method does not.

How Accurate Is the Rubric Approach?

Some noneducators, and even some educators, react suspiciously to the role that teacher judgment plays in the rubric approach to scoring classroom assessments. They assume that it introduces an element of subjectivity into grading. What these

FIGURE 4.18
Comparative Student Rankings: Rubric vs. Points System

4th Grade Teacher			8th Grade Teacher		
Student	Rank Using Rubric	Rank Using Points	Student	Rank Using Rubric	Rank Using Points
A	1	2	A	1	4
B	2	4	B	2	2
C	3	1	C	3	1
D	4	7	D	4	7
E	5	3	E	5	6
F	6	5	F	6	3
G	7	11	G	7	11
H	8	9	H	8	8
I	9	12	I	9	14
J	10	6	J	10	5

critics commonly fail to realize is that the current system based on points and percentages is inherently subjective. Citing the research of others (e.g., Ornstein, 1994), Guskey (1996b) notes that "regardless of the method used, assigning grades or reporting on student learning is inherently subjective" (p. 17).

However, a question still remains as to the relative accuracy of the rubric method of scoring assessments. Is it any less subjective than the point method? To answer this question, I conducted a study as an aid in preparing this book. For comparative purposes, two teachers each scored a specific assessment twice—once using rubrics and once by adding up points. One teacher taught 8th grade mathematics, the other 4th grade social studies. One teacher used the rubric approach first to score the assess-

ment; the other teacher used the point method first. One interesting finding from this study was that the different scoring methods produced different results. Figure 4.18 shows the comparative rankings of 10 students in each class.

As shown, the rank order for students in both classes was different for each. For example, consider the two sets of scores for the 4th grade class. The third-ranked student using the rubric score is the first-ranked student using the percentage score; the ninth-ranked student using the rubric score is the twelfth-ranked student using the percentage score.

Perhaps the most interesting finding for this discussion is that the correlation between the rubric score and an outside standardized test was much higher than the correlation between the point score and an outside standardized test for both teachers: .65 versus .31 for the 4th grade teacher, and .71 versus .42 for the 8th grade teacher. Assuming that the external test was a reliable and valid assessment of the topics assessed by the two teacher-made assessments, then these correlations indicate that the rubric method was more valid because it had the higher correlations with the external test. These same results are reported in a study by Wright and Wise (1988). They asked 43 teachers of grades 3–6 in six elementary schools to rate students on a five-point rubric regarding their achievement in specific classes. They then correlated these ratings with the students' scores on a standardized test. Student grades based on the cumulative point method were also correlated with the standardized test scores. Their findings are reported in Figure 4.19. As shown, across all subject areas, the rubric ratings were more highly correlated with standardized test scores than were grades based on points.

In summary, then, it is my strong conviction that assigning a rubric score to represent performance in specific topics within an assessment is almost always more accurate than assigning points. Un-

fortunately, it is not easy to convince a profession that has relied on the point method for decades that a different system is superior. One reason might be that assigning points and computing averages provides a false sense of measurement precision. Indeed, Carl Glickman (1993) explains that educators automatically, yet incorrectly, assume that the complex manipulation of numbers derived from adding points equals measurement rigor. It is almost counterintuitive to educators, then, that rubric-based judgments are more precise, even though they are.

My confidence in the validity of rubric-based judgment is shared by others. For example, as Wiggins (1993a) explains:

Judgment certainly does not involve the unthinking application of rules or algorithms—the stock in trade of all conventional tests. Dewey uses the words "knack, tact, cleverness, insight, and discernment" to remind us that judgment concerns "horse sense"; someone with good judgment is someone with the capacity to "estimate, appraise and evaluate." (Dewey adds, not coincidentally, "with tact and discernment.") The effective performer, like the good judge, never loses sight of either relative importance or the differ-

FIGURE 4.19
Correlations of Grades/Rubric Scores
with External Test Found in Wright and Wise (1988) Study

Subject Area	Correlation of Grades with Standardized Test	Correlation of Rubric Scores with Standardized Test
Reading	.50	.71
Mathematics	.44	.71
Language Arts	.58	.70
Social Studies	.42	.57

ence between the "spirit" and the "letter" of the law or rules that apply. Neither ability is testable by one-dimensional items, because to use judgment one must ask questions of foreground and background as well as perceive the limits of what one "knows." (pp. 219–220)

Guskey (1996b) provides further support for the validity and utility of teacher judgment. Citing the research of others (e.g., Brookhart, 1993; O'Donnell & Woolfolk, 1991), Guskey concludes:

> Because teachers know their students, understand various dimensions of students' work, and have clear notions of the progress made, their subjective perceptions may yield very accurate descriptions of what students have learned. (pp. 17–18)

Researcher Audrey Kleinsasser (1991) explains that educators have given over to standardized tests the critical task of making decisions about students, discounting the validity and power of their own judgments. Using an example from the domain of special education, she notes:

> Research conducted at the University of Minnesota illustrates the point. Jim Ysseldyke and his colleagues studied the decision-making process during IEPs (individual education plans) for learning disabled students. As many of you know, in an IEP meeting, everyone has a voice and everyone has a vote. Although classroom teachers and parents had spent the most time with the students, supposedly knew children the best, when the school psychologist or specialist presented the results of a psychological test, the teachers and the parents almost always deferred to the *test results* and to the judgments of the special education experts. In other words, the classroom teachers and parents felt that *their knowledge* about the child and *their own expertise* in assessing the child were less important, less valid than the results of the psychological test. In

effect, the parents and the teachers conceded their vote and their voice. (p. 10)

A final argument for the efficacy of rubrics can be made on the basis of their effects on student learning. That is, using rubrics as opposed to points may have a direct effect on student learning, as demonstrated in a study by researchers Kenneth Wilburn and Barry Felps (1983). They compared the mathematics achievement of middle school students who had been assessed using a criterion-referenced, rubrics-based approach to students assessed using a norm-referenced, point-based approach. The average mathematics achievement of the group that used rubrics was 14 percentile points higher than it was for the group that used points. The difference was even greater for low-achieving students. The average achievement of those who were assessed using rubrics was 24 percentile points higher than the average achievement of those assessed using points. Additionally, the "rubrics" group had more positive attitudes about mathematics than did the "points" group. Perhaps one of the most interesting findings about the influence of rubrics on student achievement was reported by researchers Lynn and Douglas Fuchs (Fuchs & Fuchs, 1986). After analyzing the findings of 21 different studies, they found that asking teachers to make decisions about students using rubrics rather than points enhanced student achievement by 32 percentile points. Apparently, asking teachers to conceptualize the classroom progress of students from the perspective of a rubric (as opposed to the perspective of accumulated points) encouraged teachers to think in terms of the knowledge and skill strengths and weaknesses of their students. Presumably, this perspective was passed on to students, who in turn improved their achievement.

What About the Issue of Time?

When I have presented the rubric approach to scoring classroom assessments, some teachers have questioned its viability because they believe it will require too much time. They rightly assert that if the rubric approach requires significantly more time than the more traditional point or percentage method, then it probably won't be used regardless of its merits. In fact, when used correctly, the rubric-based system takes no more or only a little more time than the point or percentage method. If one uses technology appropriately, the rubric approach takes even less time than the point method. (This option will be discussed in depth in the next chapter.)

Teachers reason that the point method must take less time because entering a single score in a grade book (as is done when points or percentages are used) is quicker than entering multiple scores in a grade book (as is done when rubric scores are used and a given assessment measures more than one topic). More specifically, teachers assume that if an assessment is scored for three topics using rubrics, then it will take three times longer to enter the scores into the grade book than to enter a single score.

This is a valid point. It does take more time to enter three scores in a grade book than it takes to enter one score, but the difference is less than one might think. Again, as preparation for writing this book, I asked two individuals to compare the amount of time it took them to enter one score for each of 30 students into a traditional grade book with the amount of time it took to enter three scores for each student into a topics-based grade book. The traditional grade book had one row per student. Therefore, an entire class of 30 students could be recorded on a single page. The topics-based

grade book had two students per page and required 15 pages for a class of 30 students. In both the traditional grade book and the topics-based grade book, students' names were listed alphabetically. In this informal study, entering a "total points" score for one student required an average 4.8 seconds; entering three rubric scores for one student required an average 19.2 seconds. Entering a "total points" score for all 30 students in the class took about 2.4 minutes; entering the three rubric scores for every student in the class took about 9.7 minutes.

Therefore, the teacher did take considerably more time to enter three rubric scores per student than to enter a single total point score—specifically, about four times longer. For a class of 30 students, however, this amounted to only an extra seven minutes. A busy teacher might say that seven minutes per test adds up over a nine-week grading period. Fortunately, this added seven minutes is made up for by the decrease in the amount of time it takes to score assessments using rubrics.

Recall from the previous discussion that when scoring an assessment using rubrics, the teacher does not assign points to individual items. Rather, the teacher uses student responses across items to make a judgment about students' performance on each topic addressed by the assessment. Given that, with the rubric-based method, the teacher is not performing such computations as weighting various items, assigning points to each item, and then adding up points (as is the case with the point method), rubric-based scoring actually takes less time than adding up points.

To illustrate, consider another small study I conducted with 20 teachers during a workshop. I organized the teachers into two groups and gave each group the responses of five students to a 10-item, short-answer test. One group scored the test using points. The other group was given two rubrics, one for each of the two topics addressed by the test.

It took the teachers using the points method an average of 12 minutes and 30 seconds to score five students' tests, which translates into 75 minutes to score 30 students' tests. Teachers using the two rubrics took an average of 10 minutes and 9 seconds to score five students' tests, which translates into 60 minutes and 54 seconds to score 30 students.

Thus, by extrapolation we can say that it took teachers 14 minutes and 6 seconds less time to score 30 students using rubrics than it did using points. The 14 minutes saved in scoring 30 tests more than makes up for the extra time it takes to enter scores into the topic-based grade book. One qualifying point should be made here. This study used short-answer items. Certainly, it would take less time to score a classroom test with multiple-choice (i.e., forced-choice) items using points than it would to score the same test using rubrics. However, as we shall see in Chapter 6, multiple-choice items are very difficult to construct and very limited in the types of information they can provide teachers. Therefore, I usually recommend that classroom teachers use more short-answer and essay items, which are more validly and efficiently scored using rubrics than they are using points.

Thinking and Reasoning and Communication Skills

In Chapter 3 we saw that academic achievement commonly involves three general categories of knowledge: (1) subject-specific content, (2) thinking and reasoning skills, and (3) communication skills. Thus far, the examples of topics have focused on subject-specific content only. However, the other two categories of knowledge might also be included in a unit of instruction.

Thinking and Reasoning

In Chapter 3, we identified the following thinking and reasoning skills as generalizable to a variety of content areas:

General Information Processing Skills
1. Comparing and contrasting
2. Analyzing relationships
3. Classifying
4. Argumentation
5. Making inductions
6. Making deductions

Knowledge Utilization Processes
7. Experimental inquiry
8. Investigation
9. Problem solving
10. Decision making

A unit like our example on weather might include one or more of these thinking and reasoning skills. To illustrate, assume that the unit included the skill of classifying. This doesn't mean that the other thinking and reasoning skills wouldn't be used during the unit. In fact, students might use a number of the thinking and reasoning processes as they engaged in the various activities. However, the thinking and reasoning skill of classifying would be the only one formally assessed and the only one for which the teacher would provide students with systematic feedback.

To do this, the teacher would consciously build the skill of classification into her assessments. She might decide that the following assessments would include this thinking and reasoning skill:

Homework	September 10
Homework	September 15

Quiz   September 20
Homework   September 29
Quiz   October 1

Each of these assessments would be scored for the thinking and reasoning skill of classifying along with the subject-matter topics specific to these assignments. For example, consider the homework assignment for September 15. As with subject-specific topics, a four-point rubric like the following would be used to score the assessments that included classifying:

4   Organizes the items into meaningful categories and describes the defining characteristics of each category.
3   Organizes the items into meaningful categories but does not thoroughly describe the defining characteristics of the categories.
2   Organizes the items into categories that are not very meaningful but address some of the important characteristics of the items.
1   Organizes the items into categories that are illogical or trivial.
0   No judgment can be made.

Four-point rubrics for all of the thinking and reasoning processes are presented in Appendix C (pp. 125–132).

Of course, the grade book would necessarily be expanded to include the scores on the thinking and reasoning skills that had been assessed (see Figure 4.20).

Communication Skills

In addition to one or more general thinking and reasoning skills, a teacher is likely to address general communication skills. In Chapter 3, we noted that the following is a representative list of these skills:

1. Presenting ideas clearly.
2. Altering communication for specific audiences.
3. Altering communications for different purposes.
4. Communicating in written form.
5. Communicating in oral form.
6. Communicating in one or more mediums other than writing or speaking.

To illustrate, assume that the teacher in the weather unit identified the general communication skill of presenting ideas clearly as one that would be included in the unit. Again, the teacher might informally address other communication skills; however, this would be the only one formally assessed. As is the case with thinking and reasoning skills, the teacher would include this communication skill on specific assessments that would be scored using a rubric. Rubrics for the general communication skills are provided in Appendix C. Here is the rubric for the communication skill of presenting ideas clearly:

4   Clearly and effectively communicates the main idea or theme and provides support that contains rich, vivid, and powerful detail.
3   Clearly communicates the main idea or theme and provides suitable support and detail.
2   Communicates important information but not a clear theme or overall structure.
1   Communicates information as isolated pieces in a random fashion.
0   No judgment can be made.

Using this rubric, a teacher would enter the scores on the assessments that addressed this general communication skill in the grade book (see Figure 4.21).

FIGURE 4.20
A Topics-Based Grade Book with Thinking and Reasoning Skills

Assessment Key:		
A. Quiz: Sept. 10 B. Homework: Sept. 10 C. Homework: Sept. 15 D. Homework: Sept. 17 E. Quiz: Sept. 20	F. Unit Test #1: Sept. 22 G. Performance Task: Sept. 24 H. Homework: Sept. 29 I. Quiz: Oct. 1 J. Homework: Oct. 6	K. Quiz: Oct. 8 L. Homework: Oct. 11 M. Homework: Oct. 13 N. Quiz: Oct. 15 O. Unit Test-Performance Task: Oct. 6

Students/Assessments		Topics					
		Precipitation	Ocean Currents	Measurement of Temperature	Reading Tables	Estimation	Classifying
Bill	A	1.5		1.0		2.0	
	B	2.0			1.5		1.5
	C	1.5				2.0	2.0
	D	2.0					
	E	1.5		1.5		2.0	2.0
	F	2.0		1.5	1.5		
	G	2.5		1.5	1.5	2.0	
	H		2.0				2.5
	I		2.0				2.0
	J			2.0	1.5		
	K		2.0		2.0		
	L		2.0				
	M		2.5				
	N		2.5				
	O	2.5	2.5	2.0	2.0		
Final Topic Score		2.25	2.5	1.5	1.75	2.0	2.25

Note: Final topic scores are not necessarily averages of column scores.

What About the Nonachievement Factors?

In Chapter 3, we discussed the fact that nonachievement factors are commonly included in current grading practices. Effort, behavior, and attendance are common to many classes at all grade levels and subject areas.

Unlike the three general categories of knowledge associated with academic achievement, these nonachievement factors are usually not designed into a specific assessment. Rather, they are often observed on a routine basis. We will discuss how this practice is done in Chapter 6. Given that the nonachievement factors are not tied to specific assessments, the records for these look different in the grade book (see Figure 4.22).

Note that there is an entry in every row for the nonachievement factors. Unlike the scores on the achievement factors, a teacher cannot identify the specific date on which a score was entered. As we shall see in Chapter 6, this practice does not re-

FIGURE 4.21
A Topics-Based Grade Book
with Thinking and Reasoning Skills and Communication Skills

Assessment Key:				
	A. Quiz: Sept. 10 B. Homework: Sept. 10 C. Homework: Sept. 15 D. Homework: Sept. 17 E. Quiz: Sept. 20	F. Unit Test #1: Sept. 22 G. Performance Task: Sept. 24 H. Homework: Sept. 29 I. Quiz: Oct. 1 J. Homework: Oct. 6	K. Quiz: Oct. 8 L. Homework: Oct. 11 M. Homework: Oct. 13 N. Quiz: Oct. 15 O. Unit Test-Performance Task: Oct. 6	

Students/Assessments		Topics						
		Precipitation	Ocean Currents	Measurement of Temperature	Reading Tables	Estimation	Classifying	Clear Communication
Bill	A	1.5		1.0		2.0		
	B	2.0			1.5		1.5	
	C	1.5				2.0	2.0	
	D	2.0					2.5	
	E	1.5		1.5		2.0	2.0	
	F	2.0		1.5	1.5			
	G	2.5		1.5	1.5	2.0		
	H		2.0				2.5	2.5
	I		2.0				2.0	
	J			2.0	1.5			
	K		2.0		2.0			
	L		2.0				3.0	
	M		2.5					
	N		2.5				3.0	
	O	2.5	2.5	2.0	2.0			
Final Topic Score		2.25	2.5	1.5	1.75	2.0	2.25	3.0

Note: Final topic scores are not necessarily averages of column scores.

sult in a loss of information. We will also consider the rubrics used to score these nonachievement factors.

Conclusion

This chapter has presented the basics and rationale for a rubric-based approach to classroom assessment and compared it with the traditional point or percentage method. This new approach requires a different way of scoring assessments as well as a new way of keeping a grade book. We discussed the advantages and disadvantages of that new system in depth. This new system does not take considerably more time than the current system, yet it provides for more precision in assessment and reporting. In the next chapter, we consider how summary scores are assigned at the end of a grading period.

FIGURE 4.22
A Topics-Based Grade Book
with Thinking and Reasoning Skills, Communication Skills, and Effort and Behavior

Assessment Key:

A. Quiz: Sept. 10
B. Homework: Sept. 10
C. Homework: Sept. 15
D. Homework: Sept. 17
E. Quiz: Sept. 20

F. Unit Test #1: Sept. 22
G. Performance Task: Sept. 24
H. Homework: Sept. 29
I. Quiz: Oct. 1
J. Homework: Oct. 6

K. Quiz: Oct. 8
L. Homework: Oct. 11
M. Homework: Oct. 13
N. Quiz: Oct. 15
O. Unit Test-Performance Task: Oct. 6

Students/Assessments		Precipitation	Ocean Currents	Measurement of Temperature	Reading Tables	Estimation	Classifying	Clear Communication	Effort	Behavior
Bill	A	1.5		1.0		2.0			1.0	3.0
	B	2.0			1.5		1.5		2.5	3.0
	C	1.5			2.0	2.0			2.5	2.5
	D	2.0						2.5	2.0	3.0
	E	1.5		1.5		2.0	2.0		2.0	3.0
	F	2.0		1.5	1.5				1.0	3.5
	G	2.5		1.5	1.5	2.0			3.0	3.5
	H		2.0				2.5	2.5	1.0	3.0
	I		2.0				2.0		2.0	2.5
	J			2.0	1.5				2.5	3.0
	K		2.0		2.0				1.0	3.0
	L		2.0					3.0	2.0	3.5
	M		2.5						2.5	3.5
	N		2.5					3.0	1.0	3.5
	O	2.5	2.5	2.0	2.0				1.0	3.5
Final Topic Score		2.25	2.5	1.5	1.75	2.0	2.25	3.0	1.9	3.1

Note: Final topic scores are not necessarily averages of column scores.

5 Assigning Final Topic Scores and Computing Grades

In addition to assigning topic scores to classroom assessments, one of the most important activities a teacher must perform is to assign final topic scores to students at the end of a grading period. As we saw in Chapter 4, each topic addressed in each assessment is measured using a four-point scale. By the end of a grading period, each student then has received multiple scores in each topic. To illustrate, consider the topic scores for the student Bill, in Figure 5.1.

Bill has received eight scores on the topic of precipitation, seven scores on the topic of ocean currents, and so on. At the end of the grading period, the teacher must devise a way to summarize Bill's performance on each topic during the grading period.

Probably the most common way teachers summarize student achievement is to compute an average score. For example, consider Bill's eight scores for the topic of precipitation. The average for these scores is 1.94, which indicates an average performance slightly below 2.00. The critical issue isn't whether the average score accurately represents the student's learning about this topic. My answer is that, in general, the average score does not accurately reflect a student's knowledge and skill at the end of a grading period. As you can see in Figure 5.1, Bill's final score for the topic of precipitation is not the average—rather, it is 2.25. To fully understand the reasoning behind this score, consider two theoretical issues: (1) the problem of error in measurement, and (2) the nature of learning.

The Problem of Measurement Error

One of the most well-established principles of educational assessment is the presence of error in all forms of measurement. For a detailed discussion of error as it relates to classroom assessment, see Marzano (2000). The nature of measurement error is commonly expressed in the following formula:

$$\text{observed score} = \text{true score} + \text{error score}$$

FIGURE 5.1
A Topics-Based Grade Book with Thinking and Reasoning Skills, Communication Skills, and Nonachievement Factors

Assessment Key:		
A. Quiz: Sept. 10 B. Homework: Sept. 10 C. Homework: Sept. 15 D. Homework: Sept. 17 E. Quiz: Sept. 20	F. Unit Test #1: Sept. 22 G. Performance Task: Sept. 24 H. Homework: Sept. 29 I. Quiz: Oct. 1 J. Homework: Oct. 6	K. Quiz: Oct. 8 L. Homework: Oct. 11 M. Homework: Oct. 13 N. Quiz: Oct. 15 O. Unit Test-Performance Task: Oct. 6

Students/ Assessments		Topics									
		Precipitation	Ocean Currents	Measurement of Temperature	Reading Tables	Estimation	Classifying	Clear Communication	Effort	Behavior	Attendance
Bill	A	1.5		1.0		2.0			1.0	3.0	4.0
	B	2.0			1.5		1.5		2.5	3.0	4.0
	C	1.5				2.0	2.0		2.5	2.5	4.0
	D	2.0						2.5	2.0	3.0	4.0
	E	1.5		1.5		2.0	2.0		2.0	3.0	4.0
	F	2.0		1.5	1.5				1.0	3.5	4.0
	G	2.5		1.5	1.5	2.0			3.0	3.5	4.0
	H		2.0				2.5	2.5	1.0	3.0	4.0
	I		2.0				2.0		2.0	2.5	4.0
	J			2.0	1.5				2.5	3.0	4.0
	K		2.0		2.0			.	1.0	3.0	4.0
	L		2.0					3.0	2.0	3.5	4.0
	M		2.5						2.5	3.5	4.0
	N		2.5					3.0	1.0	3.5	4.0
	O	2.5	2.5	2.0	2.0				1.0	3.5	4.0
Final Topic Score		2.25	2.5	2.0	1.75	2.0	2.25	3.0	1.8	3.1	4.0

Note: Final topic scores are not necessarily averages of column scores.

This formula indicates that any score (whether on a quiz, a homework assignment, or a performance task) is made up of two parts. The *true score* is what the student "should have" received and represents the student's true understanding or skill. The *error component* represents the part of any score that is due to factors other than the student's true understanding or skill—for example, fatigue, confusion over what is meant by a question, or luck in guessing. When a rubric is used to measure student achievement, the error part of the formula would also include judgment errors by the teacher. That is, a teacher might give a student a rubric score of 3.0 for a particular topic on a particular quiz. However, the student might actually deserve a 3.5, because the teacher read the student's responses too quickly and did not notice some parts of the student's response that indicated a fairly comprehensive understanding of the topic.

One of the most interesting aspects of the error component of a score is that it can work in favor of a student on one assessment and against the student on the very next assessment. For example, the teacher might assign a student a rubric score of 3.0 on a quiz for a particular topic when the student actually deserves a 3.5 (i.e., his or her true score). On the next assessment the teacher might assign a rubric score of 4.0, but the student actually deserves a 3.5. One time the teacher's error in judgment works to give the student a *deflated* score relative to his or her true score; in the next case, a misjudgment gives the student an *inflated* score. In fact, measurement experts assume that an error score will cancel itself out over time—the "negative" error in the deflated score cancels out the "positive" error in the inflated score.

This random nature of measurement error leads some measurement experts to argue that the average score is the score most representative of students' learning because it automatically cancels out low and high scores. To illustrate, consider Figure 5.2, which depicts a student's seven rubric scores for a specific topic obtained over a grading period. The dark horizontal line through the middle of the graph represents the student's true score of 1.5, meaning that the student's true understanding or skill relative to the topic is a rubric score of 1.5. From a measurement perspective, if there were no error associated with each assessment—that is, the teacher scored each of the seven with complete accuracy—then each would have received a rubric score of 1.5. However, as Figure 5.2 indicates, this was not the case. Assessments 1 and 2 were

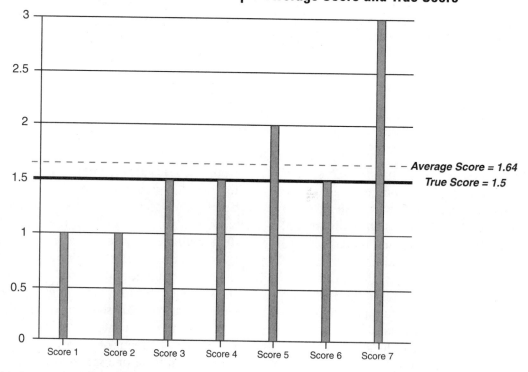

FIGURE 5.2
Seven Rubric Scores for a Topic: Average Score and True Score

Average Score = 1.64
True Score = 1.5

underestimates of the true score of 1.5; assessments 5 and 7 were overestimates of the true score of 1.5. In such a situation, the average score is usually a fairly good estimate of the true score. In this case, the average score is a very close score of 1.64.

There is one major (and fatal) flaw in the logic underlying this example. It assumes that *the true score for a student is the same from the beginning to the end of the grading period.* In other words, the student's understanding or skill relative to a topic must be the same for the first assessment as it is for the last if the average score at the end of a grading period is to be a good estimate of the true score. Learning theory, however, tells us that this is not a reasonable assumption: A student's understanding or skill should increase over time.

The Nature of Learning

Over the last few decades, research has taught us a great deal about the nature of learning (for detailed discussions, see Anderson, 1995). One of the most generalizable findings is that learning follows a trend like that depicted in Figure 5.3. The horizontal axis represents the number of practices an individual has had learning a new skill or reviewing a new concept. The vertical axis represents the student's learning with a 100-point scale. A score of 0 means the student has no understanding or skill; a score of 100 means that the student has total understanding or skill. Notice that the line depicting learning is an upward curve. Over time, there is an increase in skill or understanding. An interesting aspect

FIGURE 5.3
The Learning Line

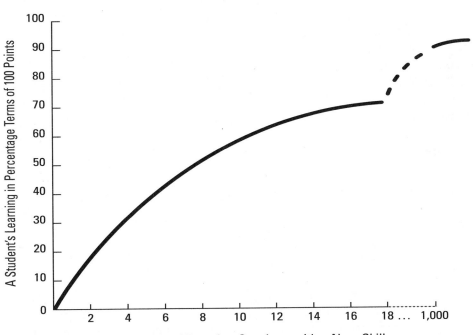

of the learning curve depicted in Figure 5.3 is that the amount of learning from practice session to practice session is large at first, but then tapers off—the learning between the later trials is far less than during the earlier ones. This trend is also observable in Figure 5.4. Notice that the increase in learning after the first practice session is almost 23 (22.918) percent. The increase in learning from the second to the third practice session is 11.741 percent. However, the increase in learning from the 20th to the 21st practice session is less than 1 percent (.802 percent). The increment in learning is less and less after each practice session.

In psychology, this trend in learning (introduced by researchers Newell and Rosenbloom, 1981) is referred to as "the power law of learning" (because the mathematical function describing the trend can be described by a power function: raising the amount of practice to a power. Appendix D, pp. 133–134, describes the formula for the power law). The power law appears to be ubiquitous, applying to a great variety of learning of learning situations. As Anderson (1995) explains, "Since its identification by Newell and Rosenbloom, the power law has attracted a great deal of attention in psychology, and researchers have tried to understand why learning should take the same form in all experiments" (p. 196).

The power law of learning suggests a great deal about the most representative score for a given student's achievement over a grading period. First and foremost, it tells us that a student's true score changes (i.e., increases) throughout a grading period according to the power law curve (see Figure 5.5).

Figure 5.5 assumes that the student's true scores follow the power law of learning. As the student learns, the true score increases. As depicted, the student's true score in the first assessment was .71, and the observed

FIGURE 5.4
Increase in Learning Between Practice Sessions

Practice Session	Increase in Learning
1	22.918%
2	11.741%
3	7.659%
4	5.593%
5	4.349%
6	3.534%
7	2.960%
8	2.535%
9	2.205%
10	1.945%
11	1.740%
12	1.562%
13	1.426%
14	1.305%
15	1.198%
16	1.108%
17	1.034%
18	.963%
19	.897%
20	.849%
21	.802%
22	.761%
23	.721%
24	.618%

score was 1.00. The true score on the second assessment was 1.24 and the observed score was 1.00. The student's true score on the last assessment was 2.21 and the observed score was 3.00. It is fairly obvious that a final topic score based on the power law is

FIGURE 5.5
A Student's True Score Based on the Power Law of Learning vs. Average Score

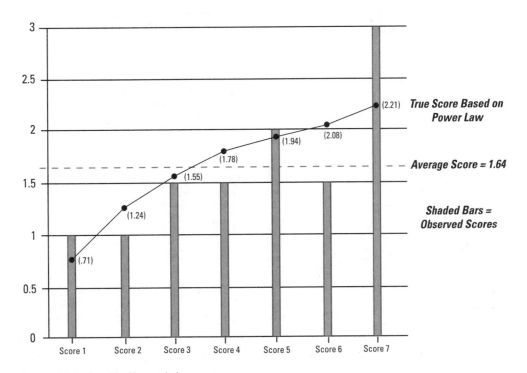

probably a much more accurate estimate of a student's true score than is the average *if* a student learns during a grading period.

One way to observe the superiority of the power law line as an estimate of students' true scores throughout a grading period over the average score is to calculate the difference between these true score estimates and the observed scores. Figure 5.6 dramatically illustrates that the observed scores are much closer to the power law line than they are to the average score. If the average score were, in fact, the true score, then the seven rubric scores as assigned by the teacher would show a great deal of error.

In short, research on learning indicates that a final score based on the power law is most probably a better estimate of a stu-

dent's true score at the end of a grading period than is the average score. In fact, this is necessarily the case if the student learns, because his or her true score will increase from assessment to assessment. Thus, the average score will be an underestimate of the student's true score at the end of a grading period.

Using the final power law score as the estimate of a student's achievement during a grading period as opposed to the average score is certainly a change from what we do now—but one that measurement experts have recommended for quite some time. For example, measurement expert Frank Davis (1964) notes:

> In some ways, [measuring individual change over time] is the most important

FIGURE 5.6
Comparisons of Observed Scores, Average Scores, and Estimated Power Scores

Assessment	1	2	3	4	5	6	7	Total Distance
Observed Score	1.0	1.0	1.5	1.5	2.0	1.5	3.0	n/a
Average Score	1.64	1.64	1.64	1.64	1.64	1.64	1.64	n/a
Estimated Power Law Score	0.71	1.24	1.55	1.78	1.94	2.08	2.21	n/a
Difference Between Observed Score and Average Score	0.64	0.64	0.14	0.14	0.36	0.14	1.36	3.42
Difference Between Observed Score and Estimated Power Law Score	0.29	0.24	0.05	0.28	0.06	0.58	0.79	2.29

topic in educational measurement. The primary object of teaching is to produce learning (that is, change), and the amount and kind of learning that occur can be ascertained only by comparing an individual's or group's status before the learning period with what it is after the learning period. (p. 48)

Because of the measurement problems associated with average scores, I strongly recommend against their use as the final topic score for a unit of instruction.

Estimating the Final Topic Score Using the Power Law

In this section we will consider a technique for estimating a student's final topic score using the power law. (For a technical discussion of the power law, see Marzano [2000].) The new generation of inexpensive computer programs, however, will compute the final power law score precisely and automatically. Later in this chapter, we will briefly review one such program. I strongly

recommend that teachers use computer programs because they totally eliminate any errors in estimating the final power law score. If a teacher has no access to such programs or no desire to use them, however, the final power law score can be efficiently estimated with remarkable accuracy.

The process is actually quite simple. The teacher simply examines the topic scores for a given student over a grading period and attempts to detect a trend in their progression. To illustrate, consider the scores for the three topics in Figure 5.7. These represent 10 scores on three topics over a grading period (e.g., nine weeks). As an exercise, cover up the bottom row of the figure (which contains a calculation of the final power law score) and try estimating it by answering the question, "Given the progression of scores over the grading period, which score is most representative of the student's learning at the end of the grading period?" Then, uncover the calculated score and see how far off your estimate was. I have found that by following a sim-

FIGURE 5.7 Topic Scores for a Grading Period			
Assessment	Topic #1	Topic #2	Topic #3
#1	2.0	3.0	2.0
#2	1.5	2.0	1.0
#3	2.0	2.0	1.5
#4	3.0	2.5	2.0
#5	2.5	3.0	2.0
#6	3.0	2.0	2.5
#7	3.0	3.0	3.0
#8	2.5	2.5	3.0
#9	3.0	3.0	3.5
#10	3.0	3.0	3.0
Final Power Score	**3.00**	**2.71**	**3.00**

ple convention, teachers can estimate final power law scores that are remarkably accurate: using quarter-point intervals.

Recall from the discussion in Chapter 4 that judgments using rubrics are considerably more accurate when teachers assign scores in one-half point increments (i.e., 1, 1.5, 2, 2.5, 3, 3.5, 4) as opposed to simply assigning whole number scores (i.e., 1, 2, 3, or 4). Similarly, teachers' estimates of final power law scores are more accurate when they use quarter-point intervals when assigning final topic scores, such as:

1.0	2.75
1.25	3.00
1.50	3.25
1.75	3.50
2.00	3.75
2.25	4.00
2.50	

To illustrate, consider Figure 5.8, which depicts the results of over 500 teachers' estimates of the final power law scores for the three sets of topic scores in Figure 5.7. The results are quite remarkable. In all cases, well over 90 percent of the estimates are within .25 points above or below the computed final power law score.

When presented with this system, many teachers have asked me why I do not recommend weighting scores on certain assessments more than others. After all, shouldn't the mid-term examination count more than a quiz? In this system, weighting makes very little sense. In fact, when estimating the final power law score, there is no mathematically legitimate way to weight one score more than another. This is not to say, however, that all assessments are the same. Indeed, they will differ in at least two important ways.

FIGURE 5.8
Teacher Estimates of Final Power Law Scores

Estimated Final Power Law Scores	Percentage of Teachers Choosing Each Score		
	Topic #1	Topic #2	Topic #3
2.25	0	2%	0
2.50	2%	28%	2%
2.75	44%	38%	27%
3.00	53%	31%	41%
3.25	1%	1%	28%
3.50	0	0	2%

Computed Power Law Scores for Each Topic:
Topic #1 = 3.00
Topic #2 = 2.71
Topic #3 = 3.00

First, teachers commonly weight one assessment more than others because it addresses more topics. For example, the mid-term exam might cover four topics, and an individual quiz only one. In the system described above, the expanded coverage within one assessment will be reflected in the number of topic scores assigned in that assessment. That is, if the mid-term exam covers four topics but a quiz covers only one topic, then the mid-term exam will be assigned four topic scores and the quiz only one. Given that a single assessment can be assigned multiple topic scores, the system presented here provides the same flexibility as weighting.

The second reason teachers commonly weight one assessment more than others is that it contains more items for a given topic, which supposedly decreases the amount of error associated with a given topic score. Certainly, a test with many items for a given topic is more precise than a test with few items. It is also true that a number of short assessments given over time will provide a better indication of a student's learning than one or two large assessments given in the middle and at the end of the grading period, because the assessments keep pace with the trend of students' learning (see the earlier discussion of the power law of learning). Consequently, I recommend that teachers try to give multiple assessments of equal precision spaced over a grading period, as opposed to constructing one or two large, all-encompassing tests that attempt to cover everything.

The Nonachievement Factors

Up to this point, the discussion about final topic scores has focused on topics directly related to academic achievement. However, in Chapter 4, we observed that a teacher might also want to keep track of non-achievement factors such as effort, behavior, and attendance. To illustrate, reconsider the scores for Bill over a given grading period (see Figure 5.1, p. 71).

Notice that the pattern of Bill's scores on effort and behavior is quite different from the pattern on the academic topics. Whereas the academic topics exhibit a gradual upward trend, indicating learning, the nonachievement factors show a more uneven pattern. There is more variation in statistical terms because performance in the nonachievement factors is more a matter of student choice than student knowledge or skill. That is, exhibiting proper behavior on a given day is probably more a function of whether the student chooses to follow school or classroom rules than whether he or she possesses the necessary knowledge or skill to follow them. In cases where student choice is the primary determinant for behavior, it is probably best to use the average score—as opposed to the final power law score—as the final score for a grading period. If you examine the final topic score for effort and behavior in Figure 5.1, you will notice that they are average scores.

That being said, a significant number of teachers to whom I have presented this idea have argued that effort, behavior, and attendance are learned skills just as much as is reading a table or understanding precipitation. My response has been that if this is their belief, and the pattern of students' scores supports this belief, then they should use the final power law score, not the average score.

Revisiting the Point Method

In Chapter 4, I begrudgingly noted that the point or percentage method could be adopted to keep track of students' performance on topics, although I recommended against it, in favor of the rubric method. Here we consider how to compute final topic scores when percentages have been used to keep track of topics.

When points are used, it is sometimes inappropriate to use the power law to compute final topic scores. An assessment may represent only a small fraction of the knowledge covered on a given topic. For example, the first assessment on the topic of precipitation might address only 50 percent of the knowledge to be covered in that topic over the grading period. If a student receives a score of 100 percent on that assessment, it doesn't mean that he or she has exhibited an understanding of 100 percent of the knowledge of that topic—only the 50 percent of that topic addressed in that particular assessment. The next assessment might address 75 percent of the knowledge important to the topic. A score of 80 percent in the second assessment would indicate that the student has exhibited competence in 80 percent of the 75 percent covered by the assessment—the student's learning has increased. However, if you were to plot the power law line, it would be going down: from 100 percent to 80 percent.

Because of the difficulties associated with the amount of topic a percentage score addresses, I recommend that teachers use the average score as the final topic score when percentages, as opposed to rubric scores, are used to keep track of student performance.

Calculating a Final Grade

Once final topic scores have been estimated or computed (using the final power law score or the average score), an overall grade can be computed. In Chapter 7, we will consider alternatives to combining topic scores into a single grade. In fact, a strong case will be made that there is no truly meaningful way to combine scores on various topics into an overall grade. In this section, however, we will assume that a teacher has no option but to report an

FIGURE 5.9
Weights Assigned to Grading Factors

Topic	Weight
1. Precipitation	2
2. Ocean Currents	1
3. Temperature	2
4. Reading Tables	1
5. Estimation	2
6. Classifying	1
7. Communicating Clearly	1
8. Effort	1
9. Behavior	1

overall letter grade and must, therefore, combine topic scores in some fashion. The most straightforward approach is to use some weighting scheme like that depicted in Figure 5.9. Here the teacher has given a weight of 2 to topics 1, 3, and 5, thus giving these topics twice the quantitative influence on the final grade as the other topics. The teacher assigns these weights before the grading period begins and communicates them to students at the beginning of the period. Upon assigning final topic scores for each student, the teacher then applies the weights to each topic. Figure 5.10 illustrates this computation for a student named Mark. Note that the quality points for Mark have been calculated by multiplying his score on each topic by the weight assigned to the topic. An average topic score is then calculated by using the following formula:

FIGURE 5.10
Computation of Total Quality Points for a Student

Student Name: Mark			
Topic	**Final Topic Score**	**Weight**	**Quality Points**
1. Precipitation	3.25	2	6.50
2. Ocean Currents	2.75	1	2.75
3. Temperature	2.75	2	5.50
4. Reading Tables	1.25	1	1.25
5. Estimation	3.00	2	6.00
6. Classifying	2.00	1	2.00
7. Communicating Clearly	2.58	1	2.58
8. Effort	2.72	1	2.72
9. Behavior	3.74	1	3.74
Totals	**n/a**	**12**	**33.04**

$$\frac{\text{Total Quality Points}}{\text{Total of Weights}}$$

In Mark's case, his total quality points are 33.04. The total weights applied to the nine topics are 12 (the sum of column 3 in Figure 5.10.) To determine Mark's average rubric score on the weighted topics, the teacher divides his total quality points (33.04) by the total weight (12), for an average of 2.75.

The next step is to convert each student's average rubric score into an overall grade. The teacher might decide on the following conversion system:

3.26–4.00	= A
2.76–3.25	= B
2.01–2.75	= C
1.50–2.00	= D
1.49 or below	= F

In this system, Mark's average score of 2.75 would be assigned the grade of C.

The cutoff points for the various grades may appear arbitrary and, in fact, they are. This is one of the greatest weaknesses of using overall letter grades. Guskey (1996b) explains that the arbitrary nature of cutoff points is a built-in flaw of overall grades.

> . . . the cutoff between grade categories is always arbitrary and difficult to justify. If the scores for a grade of *B* range from 80–89 for example, a student with a score of 89 receives the same grade as the student with a score of 80 even though there is a 9-point difference in their scores. But the student with a score of 79—a 1-point difference—receives a grade of *C* because the cutoff for a *B* grade is 80. (p. 17)

Guskey's comments also apply to the conversion system above. For example, a student who had a score of 2.08 (compared to Mark's 2.75) and only 25 quality points (compared to Mark's 33.04) would receive the same grade that Mark received.

The Role of Technology

Up to this point, the discussion has assumed that a teacher's grade book is a notebook of some kind in which teachers make entries using pencil or pen. Appendix B even includes a page that teachers can duplicate to create their own grade books. However, in this age of technology, it seems silly to expect teachers to spend their valuable time doing what can be done more efficiently and accurately by a computer. Specifically, a number of computerized grade book programs can easily be adapted to accommodate the rubric-based approach described in this book. One such program was designed by New Measure of Cedar Rapids, Iowa (http://www.rubrics.com). The software has many of the same basic features as do many other computerized grade books: course titles can be recorded, student names can be entered and quickly retrieved for each course, names are automatically alphabetized, and so on. Additionally, some of the program's features are particularly suited to the rubric approach to record keeping.

First, the program asks the teacher to identify the topics that will be addressed in a given course. As many as 12 topics can be assigned to a single course. Because teachers have total control of these topics, they can include nonachievement factors if they wish. The teacher who designed our sample unit on weather would respond to the prompts of the program by entering five subject-specific topics:

1. Precipitation
2. Ocean currents

FIGURE 5.11
Computer Grade Book Weighting of Topics

Make Topic/Standard Changes to this Class

This page is used to add your topic, standard/benchmark and the scale you will use for the topic.

Tip: Keep your Topic as short as possible.

Click on the Add button. The screen will change to allow you to enter a topic, standard, and scale. After you have entered this information click on the Save button. You will then be return to this screen and be able to see the name of the Topic you entered.

You can only assess 12 Topics per class.

Add Edit Delete

Topic-based Grade Book

Topic	Weight
Precipitation	2
Ocean Currents	1
Measurement of Temperature	2
Reading Tables	1
Estimation	2
Classifying	1
Clear Communication	1
Effort	1
Behavior	1
Attendance	1

Page 1 of 1   Finish   Cancel

3. Temperature
4. Reading Tables
5. Estimation

one thinking and reasoning skill:
    6. Classifying

and one communication skill:
    7. Communicating clearly

The teacher would also enter two non-achievement factors:
    8. Effort
    9. Behavior

Next, the computer program would ask the teacher to weight the topics entered (see Figure 5.11). The teacher's final decision is to identify the score ranges that will be used to assign grades (see Figure 5.12). Note that the program allows for 13 categories of grades. In Figure 5.12, the teacher has decided the average rubric scores be-tween 3.63 and 4.00 will be assigned an *A*; average rubric scores of 3.26 to 3.62 will be assigned an *A–*; and so on. The computer automatically provides these scores ranges as default values a teacher can select, and it allows teachers to adjust the score ranges.

The program is now set up to keep track of any assessment the teacher scores and automatically computes final topic scores and grades. For example, assume that the teacher has finished scoring the quiz depicted in the last chapter that addressed the topics of precipitation and reading tables (see Figure 4.13, p. 55). Each student in the class has received two rubric scores on the quiz: one for each topic. To enter these scores into the grade book, the teacher calls up a list of all students. The computer then asks which topics the assessment addressed. After the teacher records the two scores for each student, the computer automatically assigns these

FIGURE 5.12
Identifying Score Ranges Using a Computer Program

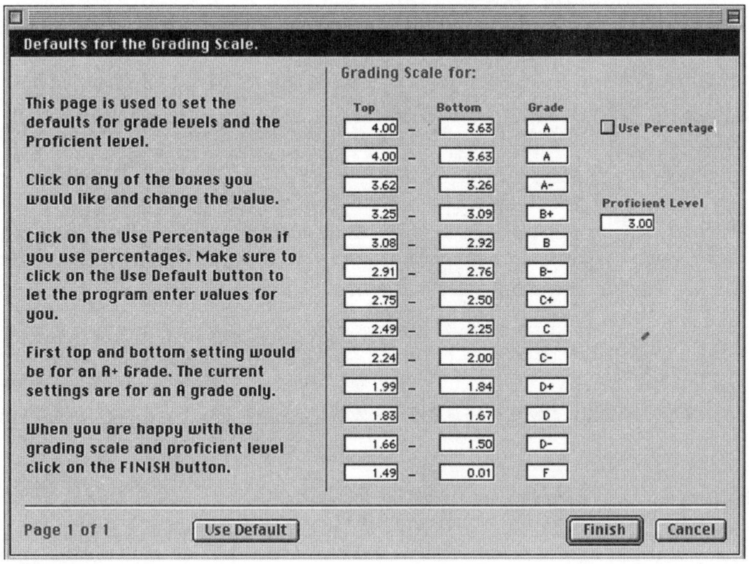

scores to the appropriate topics. At any point, the teacher can view an individual student's scores on all topics addressed in the unit, as shown in Figure 5.13.

Note that in addition to the score on each topic, the computer reports the average score for each topic and the final power law score (referred to as the "learning trend" score in the computer program). These are computed automatically by the computer based on the topic scores entered in the grade book up to that point. Each time a new score is entered for a topic, the average score and the final power law score are automatically recomputed. Finally, note that the overall grade is also reported. This score, too, is automatically computed based on the weights the teacher has assigned to each topic, the score ranges identified for the various letter grades, and the score the teacher has instructed the computer to use as the final topic score: either the final power law

score or the average score. (The teacher can also use some other score as the final topic score, if desired.) Each time a new set of scores is entered into the grade book, the average scores for each topic, the final power law score for each topic and the overall grade are all recomputed. Thus, using a computer program, the teacher need not estimate or compute any quantities. However, the teacher has complete control over which topics are recorded, how they are weighted to compute a final grade, and which quantity to use as the final topic score.

Even without a computerized grade book specifically designed for a topic-based system, most computer spreadsheets can be adapted to function in a similar way. For example, the Microsoft Excel "worksheet" can be programmed to accommodate the system described in the last two chapters. Experienced Excel users can enter the formula described in Appendix D

FIGURE 5.13
A View of a Student's Scores on All Topics Addressed in a Unit

Assessment	Date	Precipitation	Ocean Currents	Measurement of Temperature	Reading Tables	Estimation	Classifying	Clear Communication	Effort	Behavior
Quiz	9/10/99	1.50	0.00	1.00	0.00	2.00	0.00	0.00	2.50	3.00
Homework	9/10/99	2.00	0.00	0.00	1.50	0.00	1.50	0.00	1.00	3.00
Homework	9/15/99	1.50	0.00	0.00	0.00	2.00	2.00	0.00	2.50	3.00
Homework	9/17/99	2.00	0.00	0.00	0.00	0.00	0.00	2.50	2.50	2.50
Quiz	9/20/99	1.50	0.00	1.50	0.00	2.00	2.00	0.00	2.00	3.00
Unit Test #1	9/22/99	2.00	0.00	1.50	1.50	0.00	0.00	0.00	2.00	3.00
Performance Task	9/24/99	2.50	0.00	1.50	1.50	2.00	0.00	0.00	1.00	3.50
Homework	9/29/99	0.00	2.00	0.00	0.00	0.00	2.50	2.50	3.00	3.50
Quiz	10/1/99	0.00	2.00	0.00	0.00	0.00	2.00	0.00	1.00	3.00
Homework	10/6/99	0.00	0.00	2.00	1.50	0.00	0.00	0.00	2.00	2.50
Quiz	10/8/99	0.00	2.00	0.00	2.00	0.00	0.00	0.00	2.50	3.00
Homework	10/11/99	0.00	2.00	0.00	0.00	0.00	0.00	3.00	1.00	3.00
Homework	10/13/99	0.00	2.50	0.00	0.00	0.00	0.00	0.00	2.00	3.50
Quiz	10/15/99	0.00	2.50	0.00	0.00	0.00	0.00	3.00	2.50	3.50
Unit Test – Performance Task	10/16/99	2.50	2.50	2.00	2.00	0.00	0.00	0.00	1.00	3.50
Teacher Summative	10/18/99	2.22	2.44	1.94	1.85	2.00	2.28	3.00	1.77	3.23
Learning Trend		2.22	2.44	1.94	1.85	2	2.28	3.00	1.77	3.23
Average		1.94	2.21	1.58	1.67	2	2	2.75	1.9	3.1
Weight		2	1	2	1	2	1	1	1	1
Quality Points		4.44	2.44	3.88	1.85	4	2.28	3.00	1.77	3.23
Teacher Summative		2.22	2.44	1.94	1.85	2	2.28	3.00	1.77	3.23
Letter Grade	C-									
GPA	2.24									

Enter Teacher Summative – Student
Save   Cancel   Comment   Help   Default Scores
Score a single student
View Standard
Student **Aiello, Bill**   Class **Grade Book with Non-Achievement Factors**
newgradebook.com

(pp. 133–134) to compute a final power law score for each topic.

In summary, the use of computer software specifically designed for a topic-specific grade book or a generalized spreadsheet like Excel can make classroom record-keeping much easier and computation of final topic scores and final grades very precise.

Making Sure Students and Parents Are Informed

Given that the purpose of organizing a grade book around topics is to provide accurate feedback, a critical feature in the success of this approach is to make sure that students and parents are aware of the nature and purpose of the topic-based system. Figure 5.14 shows a sample letter to parents about the content addressed in the sample unit on science described in this chapter. Note that in the letter the teacher has described the topics that will be addressed in the course, the weights that will be applied to each topic, and how the topics are to be assessed.

Conclusion

This chapter presented techniques for computing final topic scores and final grades.

FIGURE 5.14
Sample Letter to Parents About Topic-Based Grading

Dear Parents:

During this grading period, we will be studying weather. To master this concept, students will have to show competence in five topics related to weather:

1. Precipitation
2. Ocean Currents
3. Measurement of Temperature
4. Reading Tables
5. Estimation

In addition, students will have to show competence in two general skills and abilities:

6. Ability to Classify
7. Ability to Communicate Clearly

Finally, students will also be held accountable for the following two areas that aren't necessarily academic in nature but very important to their learning:

8. Effort
9. Behavior

Students' grades at the end of the period will be based on these nine factors. Specifically, the following weight will be applied to each of the nine factors:

Factor 1: 17%
Factor 2:   8%
Factor 3: 17%
Factor 4:   8%
Factor 5: 17%
Factor 6:   8%
Factor 7:   8%
Factor 8:   9%
Factor 9:   8%

If you have any questions, please feel free to call.

Although computing an average of the topic scores is the most common method, we saw that the power law of learning can be used to estimate final topic scores that more accurately reflect student learning. This chapter also presented

• Ways that technology can enhance the precision of final topic scores and reduce the time needed to keep grade books.

• Methods for combining topic scores into an overall grade.

6

Classroom Assessments

U p to this point, classroom assessments have been discussed only in terms of how they can be scored using the rubric approach. This chapter addresses in some detail other types of items and assessment formats and their advantages and disadvantages in relation to using rubrics. But, first, let's revisit some definitions.

In Chapter 1, we defined *assessment* as "vehicles for gathering information about students' achievement or behavior." Thus, assessments can take many different forms. Tests are not the only viable form of assessment. True, some (maybe even most) classroom assessments will be some type of test—quiz, mid-term examination, or final examination. Yet, based on the definition in Chapter 1, any technique for gathering information about student achievement can be a form of assessment.

Three other terms introduced in Chapter 1 are relevant to this discussion. To review:

• *Evaluation:* The process of making judgments about the level of students' understanding or performance.
• *Measurement:* The assignment of marks based on an explicit set of rules.
• *Score:* The number(s) or letter(s) assigned to an assessment via the process of measurement.

The traditional method of scoring classroom assessments using points or percentages usurps the evaluation process. That is, people rarely question whether percentage scores truly represent student learning. They simply assume the scores are an accurate reflection of students' understanding or performance. Teachers do not determine whether the difference between the percentage scores of 70 and 75 represents the same difference in achievement indicated by the difference between 90 and 95. To coin a phrase, teacher judgment is replaced by the "power of the points."

From the perspective of this book, then, the percentage method does not facilitate evaluation. The rubric approach, on the other hand, explicitly builds evaluation into the process. The teacher uses the data provided in an *assessment* to make a judgment—*an evaluation*—of each student's achievement in a specific topic. The rule or *measurement* system employed is the four-point rubric. Finally, the *scoring* system used is the numbers representing the levels of the rubric.

Seven Forms of Assessment

From the discussions in Chapters 4 and 5, one might accurately infer that classroom assessments must be well thought out if they are to be used to keep track of student achievement on specific topics. A few well-planned and well-formatted assessments provide far better information about student achievement than do multiple assessments poorly planned and formatted.

Classroom assessments can take many forms. Figure 6.1 depicts various types and their usefulness to the different factors that might be included in a grade. The figure uses a scale of high (H), medium (M), and low (L). An H indicates that a particular

assessment is well suited to a particular aspect of grading. For example, performance tasks are well suited to assess processes. A score of M indicates that a particular type of assessment can be used to gather information about a given factor, but it is not particularly well suited to that factor. For example, essay questions have a score of M for process topics. They can be used to assess some types of skills and processes, but better assessments might be used. A score of L indicates that a particular format is not well suited at all for a particular aspect of grading—for example, forced-choice items are not well suited to assess process topics. Although it is not impossible to assess process-oriented topics using forced-choice items, it is very difficult to do so. Each of the seven types of assessment in Figure 6.1 have specific strengths and weaknesses.

Forced-Choice Items

Forced-choice items are certainly the most common type of assessment format used in standardized tests. Measurement expert

FIGURE 6.1
Types of Assessment Items and Formats Related to Different Aspects of Grading

Aspects of Grading	Assessments						
	Forced-Choice	Essay	Short Written Response	Oral Reports	Performance Tasks	Teacher Observation	Student Self-Assessment
Informational Topics	M	H	H	H	H	M	H
Process Topics	L	M	L	M	H	H	H
Thinking and Reasoning	M	H	M	H	H	L	H
Communication	L	H	L	H	H	L	H
Nonachievement Factors	L	L	L	L	M	H	H

Key: H = high, M = medium, L = low

Rick Stiggins (1994) defines forced-choice items in the following way:

> This is the classic objectively scored paper-and-pencil test. The respondent is asked a series of questions, each of which is accompanied by a range of alternative responses. The respondent's task is to select either the correct or the best answer from among the options. The index of achievement is the number or proportion of questions answered correctly. (p. 84)

As Figure 6.1 shows, forced-choice items are not rated high on any of the factors that commonly form the basis for grading. However, they received a rating of medium for information-based topics and thinking and reasoning skills.

Measurement experts such as Thomas Haladyna (1994) describe a wide variety of forced-choice items that include: conventional multiple-choice, matching, alternate-choice, true-false, multiple-response, and fill-in-the-blank items.

Conventional Multiple-Choice

The conventional multiple-choice format includes a stem, a number of distractors, and a correct choice. For example:

(Stem) The best definition of the term *region* is:
• A strip of land between two bodies of water (distractor).
• An area that has common political or topographical features (correct choice).
• An area of land that has a specific size (distractor).

As tools for classroom assessment, multiple-choice items are fairly difficult and time consuming to write. Probably the most difficult aspect of writing multiple-choice items is designing viable distractors. They

must be inaccurate enough to be considered wrong by students who understand the content, but plausible enough to be selected by students who are making an "educated guess."

Matching

Matching items traditionally have a form like the following:

For each item below, select the option that accurately completes the statement:

Item		Options	
A. $3 \times 4 =$	_____	1.	28
		2.	21
B. $7/6 =$	_____	3.	120
		4.	168
C. $12 \times 14 =$	_____	5.	22
		6.	12
D. $7 \times 4 =$	_____	7.	1.28
		8.	114
		9.	14
		10.	1.17

A main advantage of the matching format is that the correct choice for one item is a distractor for other items, saving the teacher time required to develop items. As the example illustrates, having more options than items prevents students from deducing correct answers through the process of elimination.

A variation in the matching format—sometimes called the "expanded" matching format—is presented in Figure 6.2. Again, more possible answers than are necessary have been provided. Along with the items shown, students would be given an answer sheet like the one in Figure 6.3. The advantage to this format is that students' knowledge of a number of factors can be probed. In the example in Figure 6.2, students must

FIGURE 6.2
An Expanded Matching Format

Person	Activity	Time
A. Lincoln	1. Led U.S. forces in Korean conflict	6. About 1770
B. Jefferson	2. Abolished slavery	7. About 1950
C. MacArthur	3. First president	8. About 1800
	4. Wrote Declaration of Independence	9. About 1860
	5. Landed in Plymouth Rock	10. About 1840

demonstrate knowledge of a significant event associated with each historical individual and an awareness of the general time period when it occurred.

Alternate-Choice

An alternate-choice item can be thought of as a multiple-choice item with two options only. For example:

An engineer who designs houses is called
A. An architect
B. A draftsman

Measurement experts explain that even though an alternate-choice item is a downsized multiple-choice item, it is not true/false. As Haladyna (1994) notes:

> Alternate-choice offers a comparison between two choices, whereas the true/false format does not provide an explicit comparison. With the true/false format, the test-taker must mentally create the correct example and choose accordingly. (p. 39)

Alternate-choice formats are particularly useful in testing students' knowledge of terms and phrases, as follows:

____ 1. A (a. noun, b. verb) is the name of a person, place, or thing.
____ 2. The part of speech used to form clauses is the (a. preposition, b. conjunction).

One of the biggest disadvantages of the alternate-choice format is that students have a 50/50 chance of guessing the correct answer.

True/False

Classroom teachers often use the true/false format. True/false items involve a statement that students must identify as being accurate (true) or inaccurate (false)—for example:

Mark F if the statement is false and T if the statement is true:
____ 1. The first thing to do with an automobile transmission that does not work is to check the transmission fluid.
____ 2. The major cause of tire wear is poor wheel balance.
____ 3. The usual cause of clutch "chatter" is in the clutch pedal linkage.
____ 4. The distributor rotates at one-half the speed of the engine crankshaft.

Person	Activity	Time
FIGURE 6.3			
Answer Sheet for the Matching Format			
A. Lincoln		
B. Jefferson		
C. MacArthur		

Teachers probably like true/false items because they appear to be relatively easy to write, but appearances are deceiving. Writing false statements is the challenge. Like distractors in multiple-choice items, false items must be plausible enough to attract students who do not know the content.

To introduce a set of true/false items, classroom teachers frequently use a stem:

Which of the following statements are false?

Some measurement experts like Robert Ebel (1970) caution against this practice on the grounds that students may look for errors only. Apparently, this subtle bias exists even when the directions read: "Which of the following statements are true?"

A final weakness of true/false items of all types is that they are susceptible to error because of guessing. A student has a 50/50 chance of correctly answering an item.

Multiple-Response Items

As their name implies, multiple-response items allow for more than one correct response. Here is one version of the multiple-response format:

Which of the following can be the end punctuation for a sentence?

1. A period
2. A comma
3. A question mark
4. An exclamation point

A. 1 and 2
B. 2 and 3
C. 1, 3, and 4
D. 2, 3, and 4

Here, students must not only identify which responses are correct, but which combination of responses is accurate. Some measurement experts recommend against this format (Haladyna, 1992) because the thinking necessary to analyze and compare different combinations of responses might interfere with the basic purpose of the item: to assess student knowledge of punctuation.

Another version of the multiple-response format is to have students indicate whether each response is correct or incorrect.

Which of the following punctuation marks can be used at the end of a sentence? Place a "Y" in front of the punctuation mark if it can be used at the end of a sentence and an "N" if it cannot.

___ a. A period
___ b. A comma
___ c. A question mark
___ d. An exclamation point

___ e. A dash
___ f. A colon
___ g. A semi-colon

Here the student simply identifies which responses are correct given the information in the item stem. An obvious advantage to the multiple-response format is that more than one feature of a students' knowledge of a given topic can be assessed. For example, the previous example provides a fair amount of information about students' knowledge of end punctuation.

Fill-in-the-Blank

The final type of forced-choice format is fill-in-the-blank. With these items, students fill in a word or phrase that makes sense within a sentence. For example,

The primary function of the cell is to

_____.

Fill-in-the-blanks are considered a type of forced-choice item because there is generally only one right answer. Thus, the response is "forced" to a great extent (Stiggins, 1994). Of all the forced-choice items, these are probably the easiest to design. The stem is simply a sentence or phrase that must be completed in a specific manner.

Using Rubrics to Score Forced-Choice Items

By design, forced-choice items are not well suited to be scored using rubrics. With many forced-choice items, the only information the teacher learns is whether or not students understand a specific aspect of a single topic. The rubrics discussed in Chapter 4, however, require judgments about

levels of knowledge for a particular topic ranging from severe misconceptions to complete and detailed knowledge. Obviously, a teacher cannot easily make such judgments using true/false items, multiple-choice items, and the like. However, if a set of forced-choice items addresses a single topic, that set, *taken as a whole,* might provide enough information to make a valid decision about the levels of understanding and skill presented in the rubric.

Some measurement experts assert that at least four forced-choice items, and ideally eight, should be devoted to a given topic as standardized tests (see Linn and Gronlund, 1995, McMillan, 1997). It seems reasonable that about the same level of coverage should be expected in classroom assessments. Therefore, I recommend using at least four forced-choice items for each topic. Additionally, I suggest the following item formats should be used in lieu of the others because they provide more information with which to make judgments:

• The expanded matching format (see Figure 6.2).
• Multiple-response items.
• Fill-in-the-blank.

Measurement expert Haladyna (1994, 1997) also offers guidelines about using forced-choice items:

1. Minimize the amount of reading time required for each item.
2. Avoid trick items where the intent is to deceive or confuse students.
3. Avoid verbatim phrasing from textbooks.
4. Avoid verbiage when writing items.
5. Avoid negative phrasing.
6. Include the central idea and most of the phrases in the stem.

7. Phrase all options in a parallel manner with similar length.

Essays

Essay questions have long been a staple of classroom assessment and, in fact, were one of the first forms of assessment used in public education (Durm, 1993). As Figure 6.1 (p. 87) indicates, essays are highly effective tools (i.e., they received a rating of H) for assessing informational topics, thinking and reasoning, and communication.

According to some measurement experts, essay items should include information that students can use to answer the essay question. The logic here is that providing students with information about details can take the emphasis off the strict recall of information. For example, as part of an essay item on the Lincoln/Douglas Debate, the National Center for Research on Evaluation, Standards, and Student Testing (CRESST) provides students with the original transcripts from that debate. Excerpts from these transcripts are presented in Figure 6.4. With this information as a backdrop to which all students have access, the following essay item is presented:

> Imagine that it is 1858 and you are an educated citizen living in Illinois. Because you are interested in politics and always keep yourself well informed, you make a special trip to hear Abraham Lincoln and Stephen Douglas debating during their campaigns for the Senate seat representing Illinois. After the debates you return home, where your cousin asks you about some of the problems that are facing the nation at this time.
>
> Write an essay in which you explain the most important ideas and issues your cousin should understand (Baker, Aschbacher, Niemi, & Sato, 1992, p. 23).

Note that the task emphasizes fairly high-level information such as concepts and generalizations—elements not easily assessed by forced-choice items.

As indicated in Figure 6.1, essay items can also be used to determine a student's proficiency with process knowledge—essays received a score of M (medium) for this factor. To illustrate, consider the CRESST chemistry example below:

> Imagine you are taking a chemistry class with a teacher who has just given the demonstration of chemical analysis you read about earlier.
>
> Since the start of the year, your class has been studying the principles and procedures used in chemical analysis. One of your friends has missed several weeks of class because of illness and is worried about a major exam in chemistry that will be given in two weeks. This friend asks you to explain everything that she will need to know for the exam.
>
> Write an essay in which you explain the most important ideas and principles that your friend should understand. In your essay you should include general concepts and specific facts you know about chemistry, and especially what you know about chemical analysis or identifying unknown substances. You should also explain how the teacher's demonstration illustrates important principles of chemistry.
>
> Be sure to show the relationships among the ideas, facts, and procedures you know. (Baker et al., 1992, p. 29)

The focus of this essay item is the process of chemical analysis. Although an actual demonstration might provide a more direct assessment of a student's knowledge of this process, research has shown that essay items can give teachers useful but not optimal information about students' process knowledge (see Shavelson & Baxter, 1992; Shavelson, Gao, & Baxter, 1993; Shavelson & Webb, 1991; Shavelson, Webb, & Rowley, 1989).

FIGURE 6.4
Excerpts from the Lincoln/Douglas Debate Included with an Essay Assignment

Stephen A. Douglas

Mr. Lincoln tells you, in his speech made at Springfield, before the Convention which gave him his unanimous nomination, that —

"A house divided against itself cannot stand."
"I believe this government cannot endure permanently, half slave and half free."
"I do not expect the Union to be dissolved, I don't expect the house to fall; but I do expect it will cease to be divided."
"It will become all one thing or all the other."

That is the fundamental principle upon which he sets out in this campaign. Well, I do not suppose you will believe one word of it when you come to examine it carefully, and see its consequences. Although the Republic has existed from 1789 to this day, divided into Free States and Slave States, yet we are told that in the future it cannot endure unless they shall become all free or all slave. For that reason he says. . . .

Abraham Lincoln

Judge Douglas made two points upon my recent speech at Springfield. He says they are to be the issues of this campaign. The first one of these points he bases upon the language in a speech which I delivered at Springfield which I believe I can quote correctly from memory. I said there that "we are now far into the fifth year since a policy was instituted for the avowed object, and with the confident promise, of putting an end to slavery agitation; under the operation of that policy, that agitation had not only not ceased, but had constantly augmented." "I believe it will not cease until a crisis shall have been reached and passed. 'A house divided against itself cannot stand.' I believe this Government cannot endure permanently, half slave and half free." "I do not expect the Union to be dissolved"—I am quoting from my speech—"I do not expect the house to fall, but I do expect it will cease to be divided. It will become all one thing or the other. Either the opponents of slavery will arrest the spread of it and place it where the public mind shall rest, in the belief that it is in the course of ultimate extinction, or its advocates will push it forward until it shall become alike lawful in all the States, North as well as South.". . .

Source: From *Political debates between Abraham Lincoln and Stephen A. Douglas*, by Cleveland, 1902, in Baker, Aschbacher, Niemi, & Sato (1992, pp. 43–47).

Figure 6.1 indicates that essays are also good vehicles for assessing thinking and reasoning skills. Recall that in Chapter 3, 10 thinking and reasoning skills were recommended (p. 36). Thinking and reasoning skills are easily integrated into essay questions. For example, an essay question about the nine planets having destination patterns and movement around the sun that elicits a student's understanding would be:

Each planet in the solar system has a unique orbit. Describe each of those orbits.

To expand this question to explicitly include one of the 10 thinking and reasoning skills introduced in Chapter 3, the teacher might redesign the question as follows:

> Each planet in the solar system has a unique orbit around the sun. Organize the planets into two or more categories based on their orbits, and then describe and defend any generalizations you can make about each category.

This essay question now assesses students' (1) ability to classify information, and (2) understanding of the patterns of movement of the nine planets.

In designing essay assignments that include thinking and reasoning skills, many teachers find the questions in Figure 6.5 useful. To use this information, a teacher simply applies the questions to specific topics. For example, for an essay question about the planets, the teacher simply applied the following questions: "Do you want to organize things into groups? Do you want to identify the rules or characteristics that have been used to form groups?"

Essay items are also useful for assessing communication skills. (Chapter 3 recommended six communication skills; see Figure 3.5, p. 36.) Given that, by definition, essay items require students to write their answer, they are excellent vehicles for assessing a variety of written communication skills. Directions need only be added to let students know that they will be assessed on a specific communication skill. To illustrate, the essay item about the planets could be altered to include the skill of presenting ideas by adding a simple direction:

> Each planet in the solar system has a unique orbit around the sun. Organize the planets into two or more categories based on their orbit, and then describe

and defend any generalization you make about each category. In your response, be sure to express your ideas clearly, because this will be one of the factors on which you are graded.

Using Rubrics to Score Essay Questions

Essay questions are quite amenable to scoring using rubrics. For the item about planetary orbits, three separate rubrics would be used to evaluate each student's response, with three separate scores provided: one for the student's understanding of the information about the planets, one for effectiveness at classifying the planetary orbits, and one for the ability to communicate ideas clearly.

Short Written Responses

Short written responses can be thought of as "mini essays." For example, each of the following questions would elicit a short written response from students:

Science
Provide a brief explanation of
1. A rock cycle
2. How clouds affect weather and climate
3. Short-term versus long-term weather changes

Math
Provide a brief answer to each of the following:
1. Represent $3/4$ in two other ways
2. Briefly describe the steps necessary to perform the following calculation: $1/2 \div 2/3$

Reading
Provide a brief answer to the following:

FIGURE 6.5
Questions Useful for Assessing Thinking and Reasoning Skills

Thinking and Reasoning Process	Related Questions
1. Comparing and contrasting	• Do you want to determine how things are similar or different?
2. Analyzing relationships	• Do you see a relationship or pattern that is central to the information? How would you describe that relationship or pattern?
3. Classifying	• Do you want to organize things into groups? Do you want to identify the rules or characteristics that have been used to form groups?
4. Argumentation	• Is there a position you want to defend on a particular issue? • Are there differing perspectives on an issue that you want to explore?
5. Making inductions	• What conclusions can you make based on what has been observed?
6. Making deductions	• What rule or rules are operating in this situation? Based on these rules, what can be concluded? • Are any rules not being followed in this situation?
7. Experimental inquiry	• Is there a prediction you want to make and then test? • Do you have a new theory or idea that you want to explore?
8. Investigation	• Do you have a hypothesis about a past or future event that you want to explore?
9. Problem solving	• Do you want to describe how some obstacles can be overcome? • Do you want to improve on something?
10. Decision making	• Is there an important decision to study or make?

1. What are some things you can do when you come across a word you don't recognize when you are reading?

2. What are some things you should be considering as you read an essay by someone who is trying to persuade you that a particular point of view is accurate?

History
Briefly describe the major impact of each of the following events:
1. Battle of Gettysburg
2. Battle of Atlanta

According to Figure 6.1, responses to questions like these are best used to assess students' understanding of informational topics. They also have some utility with thinking and reasoning skills. Their flexibility is limited by the shortness of the responses usually provided to these types of items.

Using Rubrics to Score Short Written Responses

Like essays, short written responses are highly amenable to rubric scoring. Compared with essays, however—which usually require two or more rubrics to address the multiple factors—short written responses more often than not require only one rubric because they deal with information only.

Oral Reports

Oral reports are like essays, except that they are delivered orally, not in writing. They assess students' speaking ability. As indicated in Figure 6.1, their pattern of strengths and weaknesses parallels that of essays: they are highly effective at assessing informational topics, thinking and reasoning, and communication skills.

Scoring Oral Reports Using Rubrics

Like essays, oral reports are designed to be scored using rubrics. Again, multiple rubrics are commonly used because oral reports commonly address more than one factor.

Performance Tasks

Although the terms *performance task* and *authentic task* are frequently used synonymously, it is useful to make a distinction between the two. One of the defining characteristics of performance tasks *and* authentic tasks is that they require students to construct their responses and apply their knowledge (Meyer, 1992). What, then, is the difference? Some assert that authentic tasks are more "real life" in nature, whereas performance tasks are somewhat contrived. To illustrate, consider the following performance tasks used by the National Assessment of Educational Progress (for more examples, see Educational Testing Service, 1987):

1. Students are asked to describe what occurs when a drop of water is placed on each of seven different types of building materials. Next, they are asked to predict what will happen to a drop of water as it is placed on the surface of unknown material which is sealed in a plastic bag so that students can examine it but not test it.

2. Students are given a sample of three different materials and an open box. The samples differ in size, shape, and weight. The students are asked to determine whether the box would weigh the least (and the most) if it were filled completely with materials A, B, or C.

These tasks certainly require students to apply knowledge—they are performance oriented. However, it is highly unlikely that students would encounter such problems in day-to-day life. Contrast these with the "authentic" tasks in Figure 6.6, offered by researchers Fred Newmann, Walter Secado, and Gary Wehlage (1995). Certainly, an individual *might* encounter these tasks in real life. However, the line distinguishing performance tasks from authentic tasks is a fuzzy one. For example, is the task about packaging the 576 cans of Campbell's Tomato Soup truly an example of a real-life task that students might engage in?

The distinction between authentic tasks and performance tasks is often so vague as

---

FIGURE 6.6
Sample Authentic Assessments

Authentic Geometry Task

Design packaging that will hold 576 cans of Campbell's Tomato Soup (net weight, 10-¾ oz.) or packaging that will hold 144 boxes of Kellogg's Rice Krispies (net weight, 19 oz.). Use and list each individual package's real measurements; create scale drawings of front, top, and side perspectives; show the unfolded boxes/containers in a scale drawing; build a proportional, three-dimensional model.

Authentic Social Studies Task

Write a letter to a student living in South Central Los Angeles conveying your feeling about what happened in that area following the acquittal of police officers in the Rodney King case. Discuss the tension between our natural impulse to strike back at social injustice and the principles of nonviolence.

Source: Newmann & Wehlage (1995, pp. 24, 25).

to be not very useful. Consequently, I recommend the use of a single term—performance tasks—to refer to any task in which students are asked to apply knowledge, regardless of how contrived or real-life in nature it may be.

One question commonly asked about performance tasks is, How are they different from an essay question? In fact, an essay question that requires more than recall of information is a type of performance task. For example, the essay question that follows requires little more than recall and reporting:

Describe the defining characteristic of the rock cycle.

However, if this question were modified slightly to explicitly include a thinking and reasoning skill, it could legitimately be called a performance task:

Describe the defining characteristics of the rock cycle, and then compare and

contrast it with some other cycle you know, identifying specific ways they are similar and specific ways they are different.

Essay items that require the application of knowledge, then, are types of performance tasks. However, not all performance tasks are essays. Some performance tasks do not require written responses, whereas all essays do. For example, a performance task requiring students to apply their knowledge and skill in playing the violin would not require the student to write (or say) anything.

Like essay items, one of the most powerful aspects of performance tasks is that they can be used to assess a variety of forms of knowledge. As Figure 6.1 illustrates, performance tasks can be used effectively to assess all elements except the nonachievement factors. To illustrate the flexibility of performance items, consider the following performance task, adapted from *Assessing Student Outcomes* (Marzano, Pickering, & McTighe, 1993, p. 56):

For the next two weeks we will be studying American military conflicts of the past three decades, in particular the Vietnam War. You will form teams of two and pretend that you and your partner will be featured in a newsmagazine television special about military conflict. Your team has been asked to help viewers understand the basic elements of the Vietnam War by relating them to a situation that has nothing to do with military conflict but has the same basic elements. You are free to choose any nonmilitary situation you wish.

In your explanation, the two of you must describe how the nonmilitary conflict fits each of the basic elements you identified in the war. You will prepare a report, with appropriate visuals, to present to the class in the way you would actually present it if you were doing your feature on the newsmagazine special. You will be assessed on and provided rubrics for the following:

1. Your understanding of the specific details of the Vietnam War.
2. Your ability to identify the similarities and differences between the Vietnam War and the nonmilitary conflict you selected.
3. Your ability to make an effective oral report.

As the directions reveal, this task is designed to assess students' (1) understanding of selected generalizations regarding the Vietnam War, an informational topic; (2) ability to use the thinking and reasoning skill of identifying similarities and differences; and (3) ability to make oral reports, a communication skill.

Some researchers, such as Nidhi Khattri, Michael Kane, and Alison Reeve (1995), as-

sert that performance tasks create a classroom culture in which instruction and assessment are "seamless," blending one into the other. This characteristic, note the researchers, makes performance assessment a highly versatile tool. Studies conducted by Fred Newmann and his colleagues have indicated that performance tasks generate more engagement from students from all backgrounds and engender a deeper understanding of the content being studied (Newmann, Secado, & Wehlage, 1995). Other researchers have identified similar benefits for performance tasks (see e.g., Borko, Flory, & Cumbo, 1993; Falk & Darling-Hammond, 1993; Kentucky Institute for Educational Research, 1995; Smith, Noble, Cabay, Heinecke, Junker, & Saffron, 1994).

Scoring Performance Tasks Using Rubrics

Like essays, performance tasks are ideally suited to scoring via rubrics. Again, a separate rubric should be used for each aspect around which a performance task has been designed. To illustrate, consider the task on the Vietnam War. Because this task was designed to measure three factors, a separate rubric would be used to score each of these factors.

A Note on Portfolios

Portfolios are commonly thought of as collections of performance tasks. Researchers Resnick and Resnick (1992) describe portfolios in the following way:

A variant of the performance assessment is the *portfolio assessment*. In this method, frequently used in the visual and performing arts and other design fields, individuals collect their work over a period of time, select a sample of the collection that they think best represents their capabilities, and submit this portfolio of work to a jury or panel of judges. (p. 61)

By their very nature, portfolios were used in subject areas that naturally involve products, such as writing and the arts. In the last decade, however, there have been attempts to design portfolios for subject areas that are not necessarily product oriented. For example, mathematics educators Pam Knight (1992) and Walter Szetela and Cynthia Nicol (1992) note that a portfolio in mathematics can include:

• Samples of word problems in various stages of development along with the student's description of his or her thinking during the various problem-solving stages.
• The student's self-evaluation of his or her understanding of the mathematical concepts that have been covered in class along with examples.
• The student's self-evaluation of his or her competence in the mathematical procedures, strategies, and algorithms that have been covered in class along with examples.

Although portfolios are not the best tools for large-scale assessments, they are very useful in the classroom (Winograd & Webb, 1994). I believe they are best used for student self-assessment and will discuss this option later in the chapter.

Teacher Observation

One of the most straightforward ways to collect classroom assessment data is through informal observation of students. Researcher Audrey Kleinsasser (1991) explains that teacher observation involves the

"informal conversations with students and observations of students that teachers make all day, every day" (p. 9). As Figure 6.1 indicates, teacher observation is highly effective for assessing process-oriented topics and the nonachievement factors. Reading expert Yetta Goodman refers to this as "kid watching" (Goodman, 1978; Wilde, 1996). Other researchers have cautioned that for observations to be useful, teachers need clarity about the skills they are observing (Calfee, 1994; Calfee & Hiebert, 1991).

Stiggins (1994) provides the following example of how a teacher might observe a student's social interaction skills:

A primary grade teacher might watch a student interacting with classmates and draw inferences about that child's level of development in social interaction skills. If the levels of achievement are clearly defined in terms the observer can easily interpret, then the teacher, observing carefully, can derive information from watching that will aid in planning strategies to promote further social development. Thus, this is not an assessment where answers are counted right or wrong. Rather, like the essay test, we rely on teacher judgment to place the student's performance somewhere on a continuum of achievement levels ranging from very low to very high. (p. 160)

As Stiggins' example illustrates, teacher observation is probably the perfect assessment tool for the nonachievement factors—effort, behavior, and attendance—because they are *behavioral* in nature and behaviors must be *observed* to be evaluated.

As Figure 6.1 notes, teacher observation is also effective for assessing process-oriented topics. For example, noticing a student reading a graph while engaged in seat work, a teacher might ask the student to describe his or her thinking while reading the graph. The teacher would use the interaction as assessment data with which to assign a rubric score of 1–4.

One powerful variation of teacher observation is the informal interview. Here the teacher uses this time to probe the student's understanding of a topic in ways not easily accomplished with other types of assessments. For example, the informal interview allows the teacher to pose questions like "Tell me a little more about that" or "Explain that to me again but in a different way." This form of interaction is potentially the most valid type of assessment a classroom teacher can use.

To illustrate, researcher Sheila Valencia and her colleagues conducted a study of 44 elementary students and 31 junior high school students to determine their knowledge about a few topics (see Valencia, Stallman, Commeyras, Pearson, & Hartman, 1991). They assessed each student's knowledge of each topic in four ways: a structured interview plus three traditional types of assessment (e.g., fill-in-the-blank, short-answer, essay). By far, the interviews produced more information than the other measures. In general, the three traditional formats addressed only 34 percent of what students demonstrated they knew within the interviews: "On average, 66 percent of the typically relevant ideas students gave during interviews were not tested on any of the . . . [other] measures" (p. 226). This is a rather startling finding from an assessment perspective. It implies that more traditional classroom assessment formats like forced-choice items and essays might not allow students to truly show what they know about a given topic. One of Valencia's final conclusions was that "a comprehensive view of a person's topical knowledge may well require multiple measures, each of which contributes unique information to the picture" (p. 230).

Using Rubrics to Score Observational Data

Observational data is highly amenable to scoring via rubrics: a teacher observes a student engaged in some behavior, makes a judgment about that behavior, and then assigns a rubric score based on that judgment. This is a relatively easy and efficient process. The major problem with observational data is how to record rubric scores for students. One option is presented in Figure 6.7. Note the rows do not represent specific assignments. The rubric scores in the third row of the first column for one student do not necessarily correspond to the rubric scores in the third row of the first column for another student—these scores might have come from different assessments. In this system, a student's rubric score for a given topic is simply recorded *in the next available space* in the appropriate column of the grade book. The second score for the topic of precipitation might have been an observation the teacher made, the third score might have been the quiz on September 10, the fourth score another observation, and so on. The teacher cannot tell which score goes with which assessment, just that they are in sequential order. Of course, when this system is used, the letters in the assessment key (A, B, and so on) no longer correspond to the rows in the grade book.

The advantage to this approach is that it allows for many more rubrics per topic, resulting in a more precise estimation or calculation of final topic scores. The disadvantage to this approach, as noted, is that the teacher cannot tell which rubric scores go with which assessments. Although some teachers immediately dismiss this record-keeping option because of this disadvantage, a case can be made that the limitation

FIGURE 6.7
A Grade Book Using Next Available Space to Keep Records

Assessment Key:		
A. Quiz: Sept. 10 B. Homework: Sept. 10 C. Homework: Sept. 15 D. Homework: Sept. 17 E. Quiz: Sept. 20	F. Unit Test #1: Sept. 22 G. Performance Task: Sept. 24 H. Homework: Sept. 29 I. Quiz: Oct. 1 J. Homework: Oct. 6	K. Quiz: Oct. 8 L. Homework: Oct. 11 M. Homework: Oct. 13 N. Quiz: Oct. 15 O. Unit Test-Performance Task: Oct. 6

		Topics							
Students/Assessments		Precipitation	Ocean Currents	Measurement of Temperature	Reading Tables	Estimation	Effort	Behavior	Attendance
Brian	A	1.5	2.0	1.0	1.5	2.0	2.5	3.0	4.0
	B	2.0	2.0	1.5	1.5	2.0	1.0	3.0	4.0
	C	1.5	2.0	1.5	1.5	2.0	2.5	3.0	4.0
	D	2.0	2.0	1.5	1.5	2.0	2.5	2.5	4.0
	E	1.5	2.5	2.0	2.0	2.0	2.0	3.0	4.0
	F	2.0	2.5	2.0	2.0	2.5	2.0	3.0	4.0
	G	2.5	2.5	1.5	2.0	2.5	1.0	3.5	4.0
	H	2.5	2.5	2.0	1.5		3.0	3.5	4.0
	I	2.5	2.5		2.0		1.0	3.0	4.0
	J	2.5	3.0				2.0	2.5	4.0
	K						2.5	3.0	4.0
	L						1.0	3.0	4.0
	M						2.0	3.5	4.0
	N						2.5	3.5	4.0
	O						1.0	3.5	4.0
Final Topic Score		2.5	2.75	1.75	1.75	2.25	1.9	3.1	4.0

Note: Final topic scores are not necessarily averages of column scores.

is minimal. True, the teacher has lost information about the relationship of scores to assessments. However, I do not recommend weighting scores from one assessment more than scores from another, so the loss of information might not be critical. On the other side, the added assessment data gained can greatly improve the accuracy of the estimated final topic score.

Another option is to identify specific days on which observations are made, as depicted in Figure 6.8. In the assessment key at the top of the grade book, note that five "observational assessments" (September 10, 17, 29 and October 6, 8) have been substi-

tuted for the homework and quizzes shown on those dates in Figure 6.7. On these days, teachers systematically tried to observe students. They might have set up specific activities to enhance their chances of making valid observations—for example, an activity that required students to read tables. As they were doing so, a teacher might have moved around the room asking questions to elicit information with which to make judgments about students' competence at this process.

Finally, I should note that if the computer grade book discussed in Chapter 5 is used, then observational data can be recorded with no loss of information. That

FIGURE 6.8
A Grade Book Using Observations Scheduled on Specific Days

Assessment Key:

A. Quiz: Sept. 10	F. Unit Test #1: Sept. 22	K. Observation: Oct. 8
B. Observation: Sept. 10	G. Performance Task: Sept. 24	L. Homework: Oct. 11
C. Homework: Sept. 15	H. Observation: Sept. 29	M. Homework: Oct. 13
D. Observation: Sept. 17	I. Quiz: Oct. 1	N. Quiz: Oct. 15
E. Quiz: Sept. 20	J. Observation: Oct. 6	O. Unit Test-Performance Task: Oct. 6

Students/Assessments		Precipitation	Ocean Currents	Measurement of Temperature	Reading Tables	Estimation	Effort	Behavior	Attendance
Brian	A	1.5		1.0		2.0	2.5	3.0	4.0
	B				1.5		1.0	3.0	4.0
	C	1.5				2.0	2.5	3.0	4.0
	D				1.5		2.5	2.5	4.0
	E	1.5		1.5		2.0	2.0	3.0	4.0
	F	2.0		1.5	1.5		2.0	3.0	4.0
	G	2.5		1.5	1.5	2.0	1.0	3.5	4.0
	H		2.0		1.5		3.0	3.5	4.0
	I		2.0				1.0	3.0	4.0
	J			2.0	1.5		2.0	2.5	4.0
	K				2.0		2.5	3.0	4.0
	L		2.0				1.0	3.0	4.0
	M		2.5				2.0	3.5	4.0
	N		2.5				2.5	3.5	4.0
	O		2.5	2.0	2.0		1.0	3.5	4.0
Final Topic Score		2.25	2.5	1.75	1.75	2.0	1.9	3.1	4.0

Note: Final topic scores are not necessarily averages of column scores.

is, the program allows for observational rubric scores to be entered without losing track of scores on scheduled assessments.

Student Self-Assessment

Although the most underused form of classroom assessment, student self-assessment has the most flexibility and power as a combined assessment and learning tool. Note that Figure 6.1 rates student self-assessment high on all factors.

As the name indicates, this type of assessment comes directly from the student.

Wiggins (1993a) so strongly advocates student self-assessment that one of his nine postulates for a more thoughtful assessment system is, "An authentic education makes self-assessment central" (p. 53).

Hansen (1994) notes that self-assessment is central to the development of higher-order metacognitive skills and that it also leads to the identification of individual learning goals, which are at the heart of the assessment process:

Self-evaluation leads to the establishment of goals. That is what evaluation is for. We evaluate in order to find out what we have learned so we will know what to study next. People who self-evaluate constantly ask themselves, "Where am I going? Am I getting there? Am I getting somewhere? Am I enjoying the trip? Is this worthwhile? Do I approve of the way I'm spending my time?" (p. 37)

Teachers can use student self-assessment in at least two ways: (1) on individual assessments, and (2) for final topic scores.

Individual Assessments

When student self-assessment is used on individual assessments, students rate themselves on each topic addressed in an assessment before the teacher scores that assessment. To illustrate, reconsider the science quiz introduced in Chapter 4, which dealt with precipitation and reading tables (pp. 55–56). As we saw, the teacher assigned two scores to each quiz: one representing a judgment about students' understanding of precipitation and the other, their competence at reading a bar graph. To

build student self-assessment into this quiz, the teacher would ask students to judge their own competence in these two areas before handing in the test. For example, students could do this during the last five minutes of class, using the same rubrics that the teacher uses. For student self-assessment, it is useful to restate the rubrics in first-person terminology (see Figure 6.9).

Should teachers look at the student ratings before assigning their own rubric scores? There is no clear-cut answer to this question. By scoring each assessment without looking at the students' ratings, a teacher guards against bias by their ratings. However, an equally strong case can be made that teachers should consider students' ratings prior to making their own because of the extra sources of information they provide.

Final Topic Scores

Student self-assessments are, perhaps, most powerful and useful at the end of a

FIGURE 6.9
Student Rubrics for Self-Assessment of Two Topics

Precipitation	Reading Tables
4 I understand precipitation completely and can explain it in detail.	4 I can read tables quickly and accurately. Also, I understand how they work.
3 I understand the important things about precipitation.	3 I can read tables without making major mistakes.
2 I have a general understanding of precipitation, but I'm also confused about some important parts.	2 I make mistakes when I read tables, but I have a general idea how to do it.
1 I do not understand precipitation.	1 I can't read tables.

grading period, when students have an opportunity to provide a summative account of how well they did in each topic. To illustrate, assume that at the beginning of a nine-week grading period, the teacher who designed the sample science unit on weather told students the topics and nonachievement factors that would be addressed and the weights to be applied to each. As we saw in Chapter 5, this might be done via a letter to both students and parents (p. 85). Also, assume that the teacher had given students a rubric for each topic and nonachievement factor. At the end of the grading period, each student would present his or her ratings and evidence for performance in each area. At this point, student portfolios might be used quite effectively, because they would contain a "body of evidence" to support students' ratings for each topic and each nonassessment factor. Then, at the end of the grading period, the teacher would have the portfolios, along with students' final topic ratings, to consider in making final judgments. Assessment conferences are a perfect vehicle for teachers and students to interact about their respective judgments.

Assessment Conferences

During an assessment conference, a student and the teacher discuss the student's performance throughout the grading period. Assessment specialist Doris Sperling (1996) calls this type of interaction collaborative assessment, as does curriculum theorist David Hawkins (1973). Wiggins' (1993a) notes that a collaborative approach to assessment is inherent in the very etymology of the word:

> Assess is a form of the Latin verb assidere, to "sit with." In an assessment, one "sits with" the learner. It is something we do with and for the student, not something we do to the student. The person who "sits with you" is someone who "assigns value"—the "assessor" (hence the earliest and still current meaning of the word, which relates to tax assessors). But interestingly enough, there is an intriguing alternative meaning to that word, as we discover in The Oxford English Dictionary: this person who "sits beside" is one who "shares another's rank or dignity" and who is "skilled to advise on technical points." (p. 14)

Wiggins' comments capture the true spirit of effective assessment: teacher and student jointly analyzing the student's strengths and weaknesses relative to specific outcomes.

The notion of a student/teacher assessment conference is not new. In fact, in the whole language movement such conferences have been standard fare for almost three decades (see Atwell, 1987; Calkins, 1986; Cazden, 1986; Hansen, 1987; Staton, 1980; Thaiss, 1986; Valencia, 1987; Young & Fulwiler, 1986).

During an assessment conference, the teacher presents final topic scores for the student in each topic area. Similarly, the student presents his or her scores for each topic and the evidence used to form this judgment. Any discrepancies between the teacher's and the student's ratings on specific topics are then discussed in depth. The intent is to come to the most accurate judgment about the student's understanding and skill.

The Validity of Student Self-Assessment

Some parents, and even some educators, strongly question the validity of student self-assessment. They assume that if given the chance, students will provide inflated assessments of their understanding and skill. This fear is not supported by those who have made extensive use of student self-assessment. For example, Linda Darling-Hammond, Jacqueline Ancess, and Beverly Falk (1995) report that in their experience students commonly demonstrate a "clear-headed capacity" to evaluate their own work (p. 155). Middle school teachers Lyn Countryman and Merrie Schroeder (1996) report that parents noted students' candor in making self-assessments. After hearing her child's self-assessment, one mother remarked, "I feel our child was more honest with us than most teachers would be" (p. 68). Another parent commented, "Students seem more open and honest about their performance. I didn't get the sugarcoated reports from advisors who tend to present negative aspects in a positive manner" (p. 68).

It is important to note, however, that student self-assessment is most effective when students are aware of the specific elements (e.g., topics) on which they are to assess themselves and the specific criteria (e.g., rubrics) they are to use in making their assessments (see Boud & Falchikov, 1989; Falchikov & Boud, 1989).

A Note on Peer Assessment

Peer assessment is frequently mentioned in discussions of classroom assessments (see Darling-Hammond, Ancess, & Falk, 1995; Hart, 1994; Stiggins, 1997; Topping, 1998; Wiggins, 1998). As Hart (1994) notes:

> Informal peer assessment takes place in every classroom. Students naturally look at each other's work, note what is valued and praised by their friends, and look at the samples that teachers display in order to determine what is acceptable and appropriate. (p. 62)

Although a growing body of research attests to its utility (see Topping, 1998), peer assessment might best be used as feedback to students on which to base their own self-assessments. Students might even include peer evaluations as part of the "body of evidence" they provide in their portfolios.

Conclusion

This chapter has discussed seven types of assessment as they relate to the various achievement and nonachievement factors that might be addressed during a grading period. Each type has various strengths and weaknesses. Used in a coordinated, well-orchestrated manner, though, these seven forms of assessment can provide a comprehensive picture of student understanding and skill in achievement and nonachievement factors.

7 Report Cards with No Grades: Moving Toward the Future

The overriding theme of this book is that a single letter grade or a percentage score is not a good way to report student achievement in any subject area because it simply cannot present the level of detailed feedback necessary for effective learning. As discussed and demonstrated in previous chapters, any technique used to obtain an overall score on the various topics and non-achievement factors addressed in a grading period results in a distortion of information. This inherent weakness of "overall" grades has been recognized for years (see Stiggins, 1997; Guskey, 1996b). Only relatively recently, however, have alternatives to an overall grade been seriously explored. One option for a report card with no overall grade is depicted in Figure 7.1.

Such a report card 7.1 would be distributed at the end of a quarter or trimester. Notice that this report card provides information about student achievement within specific courses but no overall grade for any course. Rather, within each course, student achievement for each standard is reported using a four-point scale. And there is an overall achievement score for the content area focus of that course.

For example, in Algebra II and Trigonometry, a mathematics achievement score of 2.13 is the average of the topic scores of the six mathematics standards covered in the course. This score provides students and parents with an omnibus measure of student performance in *pure* subject-specific content with no confounding information. The "overall" score for each course combines the scores on the subject-specific standards for that course (e.g., the math standards for Algebra II and Trigonometry) with the scores on the standards that are not subject specific, such as reasoning, communication, and effort. To illustrate, for Algebra II and Trigonometry, the overall score is 1.95. This is a simple average of all scores on all standards addressed in the course.

In some cases, however, the overall score is not a straightforward average. For example, in Advanced Placement Physics, the overall score of 3.73 is obtained by assigning the score for science standards (3.94) 75 percent of the grade, the behavior score (3.25) 10 percent of the grade, and the average score

FIGURE 7.1
A Report Card with No Overall Grades

Name:	Al Einstein
Address:	1111 E. McSquare Dr.
City:	Relativity, CO 80000
Grade Level:	11

Course Titles: Algebra II and Trigonometry, Advanced Placement Physics, U.S. History, American Literature, Physical Education, Chorus, Geography

Standards Rating

Algebra II and Trigonometry

		(1)	(2)	(3)	(4)
Mathematics Standard 1:	Numeric Problem Solving	----------1.75			
Mathematics Standard 2:	Computation			2.5	
Mathematics Standard 3:	Measurement			2.75	
Mathematics Standard 4:	Geometry			2.5	
Mathematics Standard 5:	Probability	1.0			
Mathematics Standard 6:	Functions		2.25		
Mathematics Standard 7:	Data Analysis			2.5	
Reasoning Standard:	Decision Making				
Communication Standard:	Written	---1.25			
Communication Standard:	Oral	--------1.5			
Nonachievement Factor:	Effort	--------1.5			

Mathematics Achievement: 2.13   Overall: 1.95

Advanced Placement Physics

		(1)	(2)	(3)	(4)
Science Standard 1:	Structure/Properties of Matter				-------4.0
Science Standard 2:	Energy Types				3.75
Science Standard 3:	Motion				4.0
Science Standard 4:	Forces				4.0
Reasoning Standard:	Experimental Inquiry				4.0
Reasoning Standard:	Problem Solving				4.0
Communication Standard:	Audience	1.0			
Nonachievement Factor:	Behavior			3.25	

Science Achievement: 3.94   Overall: 3.73

U.S. History

		(1)	(2)	(3)	(4)
History Standard 1:	Civilization and Society	-------------2.0			
History Standard 2:	Exploration & Colonization			3.25	
History Standard 3:	Revolution and Conflict				4.0
History Standard 4:	Industry and Commerce			2.75	
History Standard 5:	Forms of Government			2.5	
Reasoning Standard:	Comparing and Contrasting			3.5	
Reasoning Standard:	Making Deductions				4.0
Communication Standard:	Written	--------1.5			
Nonachievement Factor:	Behavior			3.25	

History Achievement: 2.9   Overall: 3.0

FIGURE 7.1 *(continued)*

American Literature

		(1)	(2)	(3)	(4)
Language Arts Standard 1:	The Writing Process		2.5		
Language Arts Standard 2:	Usage, Style, and Rhetoric			3.25	
Language Arts Standard 3:	Research: Process & Product				3.75
Language Arts Standard 4:	The Reading Process				
Language Arts Standard 5:	Reading Comprehension				
Language Arts Standard 6:	Literary/Text Analysis		2.5		
Language Arts Standard 7:	Listening and Speaking		2.25		
Language Arts Standard 8:	The Nature of Language				
Language Arts Standard 9:	Literature	1.25			
Reasoning Standard:	Analyzing Relationships				3.75
Nonachievement Factor:	Attendance		2.5		
Nonachievement Factor:	Behavior		2.5		

Lang. Arts Achievement: 2.58   Overall: 2.65

Physical Education

		(1)	(2)	(3)	(4)
Physical Education Standard 1:	Move't Forms: Theory & Pract.		2.25		
Physical Education Standard 2:	Motor Skill Development				3.75
Physical Education Standard 3:	Physical Fitness: Appreciation			3.0	
Physical Education Standard 4:	Physical Fitness: Application		2.5		
Reasoning Standard:	Problem Solving			3.25	
Nonachievement Factor:	Attendance			2.75	
Nonachievement Factor:	Behavior		2.5		
Nonachievement Factor:	Effort	1.5			

Phys. Ed. Achievement: 2.88   Overall: 2.75

Chorus

		(1)	(2)	(3)	(4)
Music Standard 1:	Vocal Music				3.75
Music Standard 2:	Instrumental Music				3.75
Music Standard 3:	Music Composition			3.25	
Music Standard 4:	Music Theory		2.25		
Music Standard 5:	Music Appreciation				4.0
Reasoning Standard:	Classifying			2.75	
Communication Factor:	Written			3.25	

Music Achievement: 3.40   Overall: 3.33

Geography

		(1)	(2)	(3)	(4)
Geography Standard 1:	Places and Regions		2.25		
Geography Standard 2:	Human Systems			3.5	
Geography Standard 3:	Physical Systems				3.75
Geography Standard 4:	Uses of Geography			2.75	
Geography Standard 5:	Environment and Society				3.75
Geography Standard 6:	The World in Spatial Terms		2.25		
Reasoning Standard:	Making Deductions			3.5	
Nonachievement Factor:	Effort			2.75	

Geography Achievement: 3.04   Overall: 3.06

for the remaining three standards (3.00) 15 percent of the grade (.75 × 3.94 + .10 × 3.25 + .15 × 3.00 = 3.73).

In short, the weights applied to the different standards to obtain the overall score might be different from course to course. In fact, if educators so desired, the report card could explicitly show how standards are weighted in each course to form the overall score.

Of course, a report card like the one in Figure 7.1 would require a different type of transcript, perhaps like the one in Figure 7.2. The columns within grade levels in Figure 7.2 represent quarters—a typical nine-week grading period. Some standards have only one score in a given year because they were addressed in only one quarter, and others have more than one score because various topics within the standard were addressed in different quarters. Recall from the discussion in Chapter 4 that some state standards are too broad in nature to be assessed precisely. Therefore, some standards might be subdivided into more manageable topics. All topics within a given standard would probably not be addressed every quarter. As Figure 7.2 illustrates, the topics within some standards would probably be spread out across a year's time. Consequently, it is probably best to summarize a student's score on a particular standard at the end of a year by computing the average of the standards scores assigned during each quarter. This factor is depicted in the column labeled "AVG" for each year.

Figure 7.3 illustrates another option for a transcript that reflects scores on standards. Note that the first column in Figure 7.3 represents an average, meaning that students have been assessed on individual standards more than once. The second column shows the number of times each standard has been assessed. For example, standard 1 in mathematics has been assessed

five times for an average score of 2.4. This means that five different teachers in five different courses independently assessed the student in mathematics standard 1. The transcript also shows the lowest score received on this standard (1.5), the highest score (3.75), and the most recent score (3.75). One of the drawbacks to this type of transcript is the interval of time it encompasses is not readily apparent. In fact, the example in Figure 7.3 would most likely cover two or three years.

An Interim Step

Given that overall letter grades or percentage scores are so ingrained in our society, it is probably best not to do away with them at this time. This is not to say that they have merit but, rather, that a school or district will probably meet a great deal of resistance if it attempts to suddenly implement a report card like that in Figure 7.1 Recall from Chapter 1 the school district that tried to change its reporting system and encountered great resistance from some community members—in spite of the district's thoughtful, well-researched alternative to the traditional system. It is also worth recalling the words of education writer Lynn Olson:

> At issue is one of the most sacred traditions in American education: the use of letter grades to denote student achievement. The truth is that letter grades have acquired an almost cult-like importance in American schools. (Olson, 1995, p. 24)

Given the difficulty involved in removing overall letter grades, I recommend an interim step: a report card that includes scores on standards along with overall grades (see Figure 7.4). Notice that the report card in Figure 7.4 is identical to the report card in Figure 7.1 except that it

FIGURE 7.2
A Standards-Based Transcript for Three School Years

	Grade 9					Grade 10					Grade 11				
	I	II	III	IV	AVG	I	II	III	IV	AVG	I	II	III	IV	AVG
Mathematics															
Math Std 1	2.75				2.75	4.0	3.0			3.5	3.5				3.5
Math Std 2	3.5			4.0	3.75	3.75				3.75			4.0		4.0
Math Std 3		3.0			3.0			3.75		3.75				3.0	3.0
Math Std 4		2.0			2.0		2.25			2.25		2.5			2.5
Math Std 5								1.25	1.75	1.5		2.0			2.0
Math Std 6			3.25		3.25	2.75				2.75	4.0				4.0
Math Std 7									2.0	2.0				2.5	2.5
Science															
Science Std 1			3.0		3.0	3.0		2.5		2.75			3.0	3.5	3.25
Science Std 2			3.25		3.25				4.0	4.0				4.0	4.0
Science Std 3				4.0	4.0	3.5				3.5				3.75	3.75
Science Std 4				4.0	4.0		3.75			3.75			4.0		4.0
History															
History Std 1	2.0				2.0		2.25			2.25			2.75		2.75
History Std 2		1.75			1.75	2.5				2.5				3.5	3.5
History Std 3	2.25				2.25		2.75			2.75				1.5	1.5
History Std 4		1.0			1.0	1.5				1.5			3.0		3.0
History Std 5	1.5				1.5	1.75				1.75				2.5	2.5
Language Arts															
LA Std 1	3.25		3.75		3.5	4.0	3.5			3.75		4.0			4.0
LA Std 2		4.0			4.0			4.0		4.0	4.0				4.0
LA Std 3				3.5	3.5			3.5		3.5			3.5		3.5
LA Std 4	3.0			3.5	3.25			3.5	3.5	3.5		3.75			3.75
LA Std 5		2.0			2.0	2.25				2.25				3.5	3.5
LA Std 6								4.0		4.0				4.0	4.0
LA Std 7			2.25		2.25				2.5	2.5					
LA Std 8							2.75			2.75	3.25				3.25
LA Std 9						4.0				4.0			4.0		4.0

	Grade 9					Grade 10					Grade 11				
	I	II	III	IV	AVG	I	II	III	IV	AVG	I	II	III	IV	AVG
Physical Education															
PE Std 1						2.0				2.0	2.25				2.25
PE Std 2		3.75			3.75			4.0		4.0				4.0	4.0
PE Std 3			2.0		2.0		2.0			2.0					
PE Std 4				2.5	2.5				2.75	2.75			2.5		2.5
Arts/Music															
Music Std 1	1.75				1.75	1.25				1.25			1.5		1.5
Music Std 2		4.0			4.0	4.0				4.0			4.0		4.0
Music Std 3						3.75				3.75				4.0	4.0
Music Std 4		3.5			3.5	3.0				3.0				1.75	1.75
Music Std 5	2.0				2.0		2.75			2.75			2.25		2.25
Geography															
Geog Std 1			2.0		2.0	2.5				2.5					
Geog Std 2			4.0		4.0		4.0			4.0					
Geog Std 3			2.75		2.75	3.0				3.0			2.5		2.5
Geog Std 4							1.75			1.75			2.25		2.25
Geog Std 5		3.5			3.5										
Geog Std 6							2.25			2.25				3.5	3.5
Reasoning															
Std 1 (CC)		3.0			3.0		3.5			3.5				2.75	2.75
Std 2 (AR)		2.5			2.5		2.75			2.75	3.5				3.5
Std 3 (Class)	4.0				4.0			3.5		3.5				3.0	3.0
Std 6 (Ded)		2.5			2.5	3.25		3.50		3.37			3.0		3.0
Std 7 (EI)			4.0		4.0	4.0				4.0				4.0	4.0
Std 9 (PS)		3.25		2.75	3.00	3.0				3.00		3.0	3.0	3.75	3.25
Std 10 (DM)			3.5		3.5		3.25			3.25	4.0				4.0
Communication															
Std 1-Written	3.75	4.0			3.87	4.0		4.0		4.0		4.0	4.0	4.0	4.0
Std 2-Oral				2.5	2.5				275	2.75		3.5	3.5		3.5
Std 5 - Audience				2.0	2.0			2.25		2.25					

Note: The standards represented in this figure are specified in Figure 7.3.

FIGURE 7.3
An Alternative Standards-Based Transcript

Subject and Standards Rated Average	Average Rating	Number of Ratings	Most Recent Rating	Highest Rating	Lowest Rating
Subject: MATHEMATICS					
Standard 1: Numeric Problem Solving	2.4	5	3.75	3.75	1.5
Standard 2: Computation	1.6	4	2.75	2.75	1.0
Standard 3: Measurement	2.7	3	2.75	3.0	2.0
Standard 4: Geometry	1.8	6	2.75	2.75	1.5
Standard 5: Probability	1.7	3	3.75	3.75	1.0
Standard 6: Functions	2.4	2	3.75	3.75	1.0
Standard 7: Data Analysis	3.0	1	3.0	3.0	3.0
Overall Mathematics	**2.23**	**24**	**3.21**	**3.25**	**1.57**
Subject: SCIENCE					
Standard 1: Structure/Properties of Matter	3.4	4	3.75	3.75	1.25
Standard 2: Energy Types	3.5	6	4.0	4.0	3.25
Standard 3: Motion	3.5	4	3.75	4.0	2.75
Standard 4: Forces	3.75	4	4.0	4.0	3.0
Overall Science	**3.54**	**18**	**3.88**	**3.94**	**2.56**
Subject: HISTORY					
Standard 1: Civilization & Human Society	2.75	4	3.5	3.75	2.25
Standard 2: Exploration & Colonization	3.0	3	3.0	3.25	2.5
Standard 3: Revolution and Conflict	3.75	5	3.5	4.0	3.25
Standard 4: Industry and Commerce	2.7	3	3.25	3.5	1.25
Standard 5: Forms of Government	3.0	2	2.0	4.0	2.0
Overall History	**3.04**	**17**	**3.05**	**3.7**	**2.25**
Subject: GEOGRAPHY					
Standard 1: Places and Regions	2.0	3	1.0	3.75	1.0
Standard 2: Human Systems	3.75	4	3.25	4.0	3.25
Standard 3: Physical Systems	2.8	4	3.75	3.75	2.0
Standard 4: Uses of Geography	3.5	3	4.0	4.0	3.25
Standard 5: Environment & Society	3.0	3	4.0	4.0	2.5
Standard 6: The World in Spatial Terms	2.5	2	3.0	3.0	2.0
Overall Geography	**2.93**	**19**	**3.2**	**3.75**	**2.33**
Subject: LANGUAGE ARTS					
Standard 1: The Writing Process	2.6	7	3.25	3.75	2.25
Standard 2: Usage, Style, and Rhetoric	3.0	9	4.0	4.0	2.0
Standard 3: Research: Process & Product	2.8	5	4.0	4.0	2.5
Standard 4: The Reading Process	2.9	5	2.75	3.75	2.25
Standard 5: Reading Comprehension	2.6	9	2.5	4.0	2.5
Standard 6: Literary/Text Analysis	2.8	6	3.25	3.5	2.5
Standard 7: Listening and Speaking	3.5	10	4.0	4.0	3.25
Standard 8: The Nature of Language	3.0	3	4.0	4.0	2.0
Standard 9: Literature	2.75	3	2.75	2.75	2.75
Overall Language Arts	**2.88**	**57**	**3.39**	**3.75**	**2.44**

Subject and Standards Rated Average	Average Rating	Number of Ratings	Most Recent Rating	Highest Rating	Lowest Rating
Subject: THE ARTS/MUSIC					
Standard 1: Vocal Music	2.0	4	3.25	3.75	1.0
Standard 2: Instrumental Music	3.3	3	3.5	4.0	3.0
Standard 3: Music Composition	2.0	4	2.0	2.0	2.0
Standard 4: Music Theory	3.4	2	2.75	4.0	2.75
Standard 5: Music Appreciation	4.0	3	4.0	4.0	4.0
Overall Music	**2.94**	**16**	**3.1**	**3.55**	**2.55**
Subject: PHYSICAL EDUCATION					
Standard 1: Movement Forms: Theory/Practice	2.3	5	2.5	3.5	2.0
Standard 2: Motor Skill Development	2.0	5	3.75	3.75	1.25
Standard 3: Physical Fitness: Appreciation	3.75	4	4.0	4.0	3.5
Standard 4: Physical Fitness: Application	2.0	4	3.25	3.25	1.5
Overall Physical Education	**2.50**	**18**	**3.38**	**3.63**	**2.06**
Subject: REASONING					
Standard 1: Comparing and Contrasting	3.7	10	4.0	4.0	2.75
Standard 2: Analyzing Relationships	3.0	10	4.0	4.0	2.25
Standard 3: Classifying	3.0	12	4.0	4.0	2.0
Standard 4: Argumentation	3.6	3	4.0	4.0	3.25
Standard 5: Making Inductions	3.8	13	4.0	4.0	3.25
Standard 6: Making Deductions	3.2	13	4.0	4.0	2.0
Standard 7: Experimental Inquiry	3.6	5	4.0	4.0	3.0
Standard 8: Investigation	3.4	4	4.0	4.0	3.25
Standard 9: Problem Solving	3.2	5	4.0	4.0	2.75
Standard 10: Decision Making	3.6	8	4.0	4.0	2.75
Overall Reasoning	**3.4**	**83**	**4.0**	**4.0**	**2.73**
Subject: COMMUNICATION					
Standard 1: Written	2.8	17	3.75	3.75	2.5
Standard 2: Oral	3.1	17	4.0	4.0	2.75
Standard 3: Other Mediums	2.7	14	3.5	3.75	2.25
Standard 4: Ideas Clearly	2.6	13	3.75	3.0	1.0
Standard 5: Audiences	3.0	10	3.5	4.0	2.5
Standard 6: Purposes	3.2	10	3.25	4.0	2.75
Overall Communication	**2.9**	**81**	**3.63**	**3.75**	**2.29**
Subject: NONACHIEVEMENT FACTORS					
Standard 1: Effort	2.8	17	3.75	3.75	2.5
Standard 2: Behavior	3.1	17	4.0	4.0	2.75
Standard 3: Attendance	2.7	14	3.5	3.75	2.25
Overall Nonachievement Factor	**2.86**	**48**	**3.75**	**3.83**	**2.5**
All Subject Areas Combined	**2.93**	**359**	**3.46**	**3.72**	**2.37**

FIGURE 7.4
A Report Card with Overall Grades and Standards

Name:	Al Einstein	**Course Titles:**	**Grade**	**Course Titles:**	**Grade**
Address:	1111 E. McSquare Dr.	Algebra II and Trigonometry	C	Chorus	B
City:	Relativity, CO 80000	Advanced Placement Physics	A	Geography	B
Grade Level:	11	U.S. History	B	**Current GPA:**	2.95
		American Literature	C	**Cumulative GPA:**	3.23
		Physical Education	B		

Standards Rating

Algebra II and Trigonometry

		(1)	(2)	(3)	(4)
Mathematics Standard 1:	Numeric Problem Solving	------------1.75			
Mathematics Standard 2:	Computation				
Mathematics Standard 3:	Measurement	--------------------------2.5			
Mathematics Standard 4:	Geometry	---------------------------------2.75			
Mathematics Standard 5:	Probability	--------------------------2.5			
Mathematics Standard 6:	Functions	1.0			
Mathematics Standard 7:	Data Analysis	----------------------2.25			
Reasoning Standard:	Decision Making	--------------------------2.5			
Communication Standard:	Written	---1.25			
Communication Standard:	Oral	--------1.5			
Nonachievement Factor:	Effort	--------1.5			

Mathematics Achievement: 2.13   Overall: 1.95

Advanced Placement Physics

		(1)	(2)	(3)	(4)
Science Standard 1:	Structure/Properties of Matter				---4.0
Science Standard 2:	Energy Types				---3.75
Science Standard 3:	Motion				---4.0
Science Standard 4:	Forces				---4.0
Reasoning Standard:	Experimental Inquiry				---4.0
Reasoning Standard:	Problem Solving				---4.0
Communication Standard:	Audience	1.0			
Nonachievement Factor:	Behavior				--3.25

Science Achievement: 3.94   Overall: 3.73

U.S. History

		(1)	(2)	(3)	(4)
History Standard 1:	Civilization and Society	------------------2.0			
History Standard 2:	Exploration & Colonization			----------------------------------3.25	
History Standard 3:	Revolution and Conflict				---4.0
History Standard 4:	Industry and Commerce		--------------------------------2.75		
History Standard 5:	Forms of Government		--------------------------2.5		
Reasoning Standard:	Comparing and Contrasting			---3.5	
Reasoning Standard:	Making Deductions				---4.0
Communication Standard:	Written	---------1.5			
Nonachievement Factor:	Behavior			----------------------------------3.25	

History Achievement: 2.9   Overall: 3.0

American Literature — Standards Rating

		(1)	(2)	(3)	(4)
Language Arts Standard 1:	The Writing Process		2.5		
Language Arts Standard 2:	Usage, Style, and Rhetoric			3.25	
Language Arts Standard 3:	Research: Process & Product				3.75
Language Arts Standard 4:	The Reading Process				
Language Arts Standard 5:	Reading Comprehension				
Language Arts Standard 6:	Literary/Text Analysis		2.5		
Language Arts Standard 7:	Listening and Speaking		2.25		
Language Arts Standard 8:	The Nature of Language				
Language Arts Standard 9:	Literature	1.25			
Reasoning Standard:	Analyzing Relationships				3.75
Nonachievement Factor:	Attendance		2.5		
Nonachievement Factor:	Behavior		2.5		

Lang. Arts Achievement: 2.58   Overall: 2.65

Physical Education — Standards Rating

		(1)	(2)	(3)	(4)
Physical Education Standard 1:	Move't Forms: Theory & Pract.		2.25		
Physical Education Standard 2:	Motor Skill Development				3.75
Physical Education Standard 3:	Physical Fitness: Appreciation			3.0	
Physical Education Standard 4:	Physical Fitness: Application		2.5		
Reasoning Standard:	Problem Solving			3.25	
Nonachievement Factor:	Attendance			2.75	
Nonachievement Factor:	Behavior		2.5		
Nonachievement Factor:	Effort	1.5			

Phys. Ed. Achievement: 2.88   Overall: 2.75

Chorus — Standards Rating

		(1)	(2)	(3)	(4)
Music Standard 1:	Vocal Music				3.75
Music Standard 2:	Instrumental Music				3.75
Music Standard 3:	Music Composition			3.25	
Music Standard 4:	Music Theory		2.25		
Music Standard 5:	Music Appreciation				4.0
Reasoning Standard:	Classifying			2.75	
Communication Factor:	Written			3.25	

Music Achievement: 3.4   Overall: 3.33

Geography — Standards Rating

		(1)	(2)	(3)	(4)
Geography Standard 1:	Places and Regions		2.25		
Geography Standard 2:	Human Systems			3.5	
Geography Standard 3:	Physical Systems				3.75
Geography Standard 4:	Uses of Geography			2.75	
Geography Standard 5:	Environment and Society				3.75
Geography Standard 6:	The World in Spatial Terms		2.25		
Reasoning Standard:	Making Deductions			3.5	
Nonachievement Factor:	Effort			2.75	

Geography Achievement: 3.04   Overall: 3.06

includes overall grades—*A*, *B*, and so on—along with individual scores on standards. This type of report card provides students and parents with the specific feedback so necessary for learning, but it also gives them something with which they are highly familiar and comfortable: grades.

Once parents and students become familiar with this format, the school or district can move to the report card format depicted in Figure 7.5, which provides three grades in each course. One grade is an overall grade, the second is based on academic standards, and the third is based on the nonachievement or nonacademic factors. This breakdown is also reflected in the standards scores within each course. To illustrate, consider Algebra II and Trigonometry. The student's score for academic achievement is 2.75. It is the average of the scores on all academic standards addressed in the course: problem solving, measurement, functions, and data analysis. The student's score for the nonacademic factors is 3.67. It is the average for effort, behavior, and attendance. The overall score (3.21) is the simple average of the academic and nonacademic scores. A school might choose to weight the academic and nonacademic scores differentially. For example, the school might have decided that 75 percent of the grade is based on the academic score and 25 percent on the nonacademic score in each class. As discussed in the next section on changing the culture of the school or district, this is one of the many decisions that must be made when developing more precise and informative grading and reporting systems.

The report card shown in Figure 7.5 is a simple, yet powerful, step to make in reporting because it begins to send the message that putting everything into one grade makes little sense. Once students and parents accept the idea of more than one

grade, they are well on their way to seeing the logic in making reporting as specific as possible.

Changing the Culture of Your School or District

This book has presented some radical ideas that require significant changes in school practices. These changes will not occur overnight. Therefore, I recommend that a school or district take four steps to gradually change grading and reporting practices.

1. Survey Staff Members

One of the first things that a school or district can do is to survey its staff members. In Chapter 2, I briefly mentioned an informal study I conducted with educators across the country. Specifically, in preparing this book, I surveyed K–12 educators about

1. The purpose of grades
   a. For administrative decisions
   b. To give students feedback about their achievement
   c. To give students guidance about future course work
   d. To help teachers in instructional planning
   e. To motivate students

2. The referent for grades
   a. A predetermined distribution of scores (i.e., a norm-referenced system)
   b. Specific learning objectives (i.e., a criterion-referenced system)
   c. Knowledge gain

3. The factors that should be included in grades
   a. Academic achievement
   b. Effort

FIGURE 7.5
A Report Card with Academic and Nonacademic Grades

		Course Title	Overall	Academic	Nonacademic
Name:	Al Einstein	Algebra II & Trigonometry	B+	C	A
Address:	1111 E. McSquare Dr.	Advanced Placement Physics	A	A	B
City:	Relativity, CO 80000	U.S. History	C+	B	C
Grade Level:	11	American Literature	A	A	A
Quarter:	Fourth	Physical Education	A–	A	B+
		Chorus	B–	C	A
		Geography	B	B	B
		Current GPA:	**3.33**	**3.24**	**3.43**

Standards Rating

Algebra II & Trigonometry		(1)	(2)	(3)	(4)
Mathematics Standard 1:	Numeric Problem Solving		2.5		
Mathematics Standard 2:	Computation				
Mathematics Standard 3:	Measurement			3.0	
Mathematics Standard 4:	Geometry				
Mathematics Standard 5:	Probability				
Mathematics Standard 6:	Functions			3.0	
Mathematics Standard 7:	Data Analysis		2.5		
Reasoning Standard:	Decision Making				
Communication Standard:	Written				
Communication Standard:	Oral				
Nonachievement Factor:	Effort			3.5	
Nonachievement Factor:	Behavior				4.0
Nonachievement Factor:	Attendance			3.5	
Academic: 2.75	**Overall: 3.21**	**Nonacademic: 3.67**			

Advanced Placement Physics		(1)	(2)	(3)	(4)
Science Standard 1:	Structure/Properties of Matter			3.5	
Science Standard 2:	Energy Types				4.0
Science Standard 3:	Motion				4.0
Science Standard 4:	Forces			3.75	
Reasoning Standard:	Experimental Inquiry				4.0
Reasoning Standard:	Problem Solving				
Communication Standard:	Audience				
Communication Standard:	Oral				
Nonachievement Factor:	Effort			3.75	
Nonachievement Factor:	Behavior			3.0	
Nonachievement Factor:	Attendance			3.0	
Academic: 3.85	**Overall: 3.55**	**Nonacademic: 3.25**			

U.S. History		(1)	(2)	(3)	(4)
History Standard 1:	Civilization and Society				
History Standard 2:	Exploration & Colonization			3.5	
History Standard 3:	Revolution and Conflict	1.5			
History Standard 4:	Industry and Commerce				
History Standard 5:	Forms of Government		2.5		
Reasoning Standard:	Comparing and Contrasting		2.75		
Reasoning Standard:	Problem Solving				4.0
Communication Standard:	Written				
Nonachievement Factor:	Effort			3.0	
Nonachievement Factor:	Behavior	1.75			
Nonachievement Factor:	Attendance		2.25		
Academic: 2.85	**Overall: 2.59**	**Nonacademic: 2.33**			

FIGURE 7.5 *(continued)*

American Literature	Standards Rating			
	(1)	(2)	(3)	(4)
Language Arts Standard 1: The Writing Process				4.0
Language Arts Standard 2: Usage, Style, and Rhetoric				
Language Arts Standard 3: Research: Process and Product				
Language Arts Standard 4: The Reading Process				
Language Arts Standard 5: Reading Comprehension			3.5	
Language Arts Standard 6: Literary/Text Analysis				4.0
Language Arts Standard 7: Listening and Speaking				
Language Arts Standard 8: The Nature of Language			3.5	
Language Arts Standard 9: Literature				
Reasoning Standard: Analyzing Relationships				
Nonachievement Factor: Effort				4.0
Nonachievement Factor: Behavior				4.0
Nonachievement Factor: Attendance				4.0

Academic: 3.75 **Overall: 3.88** **Nonacademic: 4.0**

Physical Education	Standards Rating			
	(1)	(2)	(3)	(4)
Physical Education Standard 1: Movement Forms: Theory/Practice				
Physical Education Standard 2: Motor Skill Development				4.0
Physical Education Standard 3: Physical Fitness: Appreciation				4.0
Physical Education Standard 4: Physical Fitness: Application				4.0
Reasoning Standard: Problem Solving				
Nonachievement Factor: Effort			3.75	
Nonachievement Factor: Behavior		2.75		
Nonachievement Factor: Attendance				4.0

Academic: 4.0 **Overall: 3.75** **Nonacademic: 3.5**

Chorus	Standards Rating			
	(1)	(2)	(3)	(4)
Music Standard 1: Vocal Music	1.5			
Music Standard 2: Instrumental Music				
Music Standard 3: Music Composition				4.0
Music Standard 4: Music Theory	1.75			
Music Standard 5: Music Appreciation				
Reasoning Standard: Classifying			3.0	
Communication Factor: Written				
Nonachievement Factor: Effort				4.0
Nonachievement Factor: Behavior				4.0
Nonachievement Factor: Attendance				4.0

Academic: 2.56 **Overall: 3.28** **Nonacademic: 4.0**

Geography	Standards Rating			
	(1)	(2)	(3)	(4)
Geography Standard 1: Places and Regions				
Geography Standard 2: Human Systems				
Geography Standard 3: Physical Systems		2.5		
Geography Standard 4: Uses of Geography				
Geography Standard 5: Environment and Society				
Geography Standard 6: The World in Spatial Terms			3.5	
Reasoning Standard: Making Deductions				
Nonachievement Factor: Effort		2.25		
Nonachievement Factor: Behavior			3.5	
Nonachievement Factor: Attendance				4.0

Academic: 3.0 **Overall: 3.13** **Nonacademic: 3.25**

c. Behavior

d. Attendance

These topics, as discussed in Chapters 2 and 3, are critical to the design of an effective system of grading. The questionnaire used in my informal study is reported in Figure 7.6 and again in Appendix A. That questionnaire can be duplicated or adapted by schools and districts to survey their teachers.

I refer to my study as informal because the teachers and administrators surveyed were not randomly selected but were participants in workshops I have conducted across the country. Consequently, the results (shown in Figure 7.7) may not represent the opinions of teachers and administrators in general.

Certain patterns of response related to these issues, however, are good indicators that a school or district is ready for some or all of the changes described in this book. For example, if a majority of educators report that the purpose of grades is to provide feedback to students and parents, that school or district is open to the changes in this book. To illustrate, consider the responses to my informal survey in Part I of Figure 7.7 (78 percent of teachers and 83 percent of administrators scored this item a 4).

Survey results indicating a readiness for change would be those in which the majority of teachers favor a criterion-referenced system. The results of my informal survey on this issue are reported in Part II of Figure 7.7. Clearly, the majority of teachers (62%) and administrators (59%) preferred a criterion-referenced grading system.

Finally, any response pattern relative to Part III of the questionnaire is consistent with the recommendations in this book. That is, the recommendations will work whether a school or district decides that grades should focus on academic achievement, the nonachievement factors of effort, behavior, and attendance, or both. As depicted in Part III of Figure 7.7, teachers (89%) and administrators (94%) assigned academic achievement a score of 4 in the questionnaire.

2. Obtain Agreement on What Factors Will Be Included in Grades

Individual teachers can use the system described in this book to implement their personal grading schemes in a more precise manner than allowed by the point system. However, for a school or district to have a truly effective grading policy, certain aspects of grading must be school or district policy. Specifically, a school or district should not only identify which of the nonachievement factors will be included in grades, but also which subject-matter content, thinking and reasoning skills, and general communication skills will be included.

3. Obtain Agreement on the Weights That Will Be Applied

Once agreement has been reached on the factors that will be included in grades, the next step is to agree on the weights to apply to those factors. In informal discussions with teachers and administrators, I have found that this issue can be somewhat contentious. Whereas some educators will vehemently assert that effort (let's say) should count for 50 percent of an overall grade, other educators will just as forcefully assert that it should count for 10 percent. As difficult as it might be to resolve these differences, I strongly urge that schools and districts do whatever it takes to do so. Once

FIGURE 7.6
Teacher and Administrator Survey Questions About Grading and Reporting Practices

Part I: Purpose of Grades	Not at All———————To a Great Extent			
1. *Administrative:* To what extent should grades be used to make administrative decisions such as whether students progress to the next grade level, class rank, whether credits are earned, and so on?	1	2	3	4
2. *Feedback:* To what extent should grades be used to provide students and parents with feedback about student learning?	1	2	3	4
3. *Guidance:* To what extent should grades be used to provide students with guidance relative to courses they should take, occupations they should consider, and so on?	1	2	3	4
4. *Instructional planning:* To what extent should grades be used to plan instruction?	1	2	3	4
5. *Motivation:* To what extent should grades be used to motivate students?	1	2	3	4

Part II: Reference Point for Grades

Which of the following is the most appropriate referencing system for grades:

Norm-Referencing? ____

Criterion-Referencing? ____

Referencing to Knowledge Gain? ____

Part III: Basis for Grades	Not at All———————To a Great Extent			
1. *Academic Achievement:* To what extent should academic achievement be used as the basis for grades?	1	2	3	4
2. *Effort:* To what extent should effort be used as the basis for grades?	1	2	3	4
3. *Behavior:* To what extent should behavior be used as the basis for grades?	1	2	3	4
4. *Attendance:* To what extent should attendance be used as the basis for grades?	1	2	3	4

FIGURE 7.7
Teacher and Administrator Responses to Survey Questions
About Grading and Reporting Practices

Part I: Purpose of Grades	Teachers				Administrators			
	Scoring Levels Not at All—To a Great Extent				Scoring Levels Not at All—To a Great Extent			
	1	2	3	4	1	2	3	4
Question Topics	Percentage of Responses				Percentage of Responses			
Administrative	6%	37%	28%	29%	0%	5%	47%	48%
Feedback	0%	2%	20%	78%	0%	3%	14%	83%
Guidance	25%	42%	21%	12%	4%	18%	48%	30%
Instructional Planning	12%	34%	33%	21%	21%	29%	31%	19%
Motivation	3%	17%	34%	46%	12%	28%	36%	24%

Part II: Reference for Grades	Percentage of Teachers' Responses	Percentage of Administrators' Responses
Norm-Referencing	7%	12%
Criterion-Referencing	62%	59%
Referencing to Knowledge Gain	31%	29%

Part III: Basis for Grades	Teachers				Administrators			
	Scoring Levels Not at All——To a Great Extent				Scoring Levels Not at All—To a Great Extent			
	1	2	3	4	1	2	3	4
Question Topics	Percentages of Responses				Percentages of Responses			
Academic Achievement	0%	2%	9%	89%	0%	0%	6%	94%
Effort	17%	13%	32%	48%	18%	24%	29%	29%
Behavior	2%	34%	23%	22%	35%	28%	26%	11%
Attendance	41%	30%	19%	10%	47%	36%	12%	5%

Note: The percentages reported here are based on responses of over 300 teachers and 150 administrators.

agreement is reached, a school or district is in a position to communicate its values powerfully to students and parents precisely because of the commonality in grading practices.

4. Gradually Change the Report Card

Someday I hope to see report cards with no overall grades. The first step in this journey is to implement a report card with overall grades in addition to scores on individual standards or topics, like that shown in Figure 7.4. The next step might be to move to a report card with two grades for each course—one for academic content and one for the nonacademic factors—as illustrated in Figure 7.5. Finally, a report card like that in Figure 7.1 can be introduced—one that has no overall grades, only individual scores for specific standards and specific nonachievement factors. By virtue of the preparation provided by the first two report card formats (Figure 7.4 and 7.5), this new format with no overall grades should meet with little resistance, and some schools may even make the change with great enthusiasm.

Conclusion

This book has presented a new way of approaching grading and reporting. Schools and districts that systematically implement the changes recommended in this book will fundamentally change the way teachers, students, and parents think about and use grading. Grading can become a tool for all to use in pinpointing strengths and weaknesses in students' understanding. It can clarify expectations, and it can provide a shared language for discussing students' learning. Most important, a carefully developed grading system can help us *improve* student performance over time rather than simply label it at periodic intervals.

Finally, I should note that I am fully aware of the fact that the changes identified in this book will not come easily. In fact, it might be accurate to say that these changes will require a certain amount of persistence, even courage, on the part of educators. I sincerely encourage those in positions to facilitate these changes to stay the course. While presenting the ideas embodied in this text to virtually thousands of educators across the country, I have come to the conclusion that their time has come. Individual teachers, schools, and districts stand poised for action: they are ready for change. What is required now is for some members of that group to take the lead—to be the vanguard. I hope this book will provide explicit guidance for those teachers, schools, and districts.

APPENDIX A Survey Questions About Grading and Reporting Practices

Part I: Purpose of Grades	Not at All————————To a Great Extent			
1. *Administrative:* To what extent should grades be used to make administrative decisions such as whether students progress to the next grade level, class rank, whether credits are earned, and so on?	1	2	3	4
2. *Feedback:* To what extent should grades be used to provide students and parents with feedback about student learning?	1	2	3	4
3. *Guidance:* To what extent should grades be used to provide students with guidance relative to courses they should take, occupations they should consider, and so on?	1	2	3	4
4. *Instructional planning:* To what extent should grades be used to plan instruction?	1	2	3	4
5. *Motivation:* To what extent should grades be used to motivate students?	1	2	3	4

Part II: Reference Point for Grades

Which of the following is the most appropriate referencing system for grades:

        Norm-Referencing?   _____

        Criterion-Referencing?   _____

        Referencing to Knowledge Gain?   _____

Part III: Basis for Grades	Not at All————————To a Great Extent			
1. *Academic Achievement:* To what extent should academic achievement be used as the basis for grades?	1	2	3	4
2. *Effort:* To what extent should effort be used as the basis for grades?	1	2	3	4
3. *Behavior:* To what extent should behavior be used as the basis for grades?	1	2	3	4
4. *Attendance:* To what extent should attendance be used as the basis for grades?	1	2	3	4

APPENDIX B | A Sample Grade Book Page

Assessment Key:	A. B. C. D. E.		F. G. H. I. J.		K. L. M. N. O.
Students/Assessments	**Topics**				
	A				
	B				
	C				
	D				
	E				
	F				
	G				
	H				
	I				
	J				
	K				
	L				
	M				
	N				
	O				
Final Topic Score					
	A				
	B				
	C				
	D				
	E				
	F				
	G				
	H				
	I				
	J				
	K				
	L				
	M				
	N				
	O				
Final Topic Score					

Source: Marzano & Kendall (1996). Copyright © 1996 by McREL Institute. Reprinted by permission.

APPENDIX **C** Rubrics

Information-Based Topics

4   The student has a complete and detailed understanding of the information important to the topic.

3   The student has a complete understanding of the information important to the topic but not in great detail.

2   The student has an incomplete understanding of the topic and/or misconceptions about some of the information. However, the student maintains a basic understanding of the topic.

1   The student's understanding of the topic is so incomplete or has so many misconceptions that the student cannot be said to understand the topic.

0   No judgment can be made.

Skill- or Process-Based Topics

4   The student can perform the skill or process important to the topic with no significant errors and with fluency. Additionally, the student understands the key features of the skill process.

3   The student can perform the skill or process important to the topic without making significant errors.

2   The student makes some significant errors when performing the skill or process important to the topic but still accomplishes a rough approximation of the skill or process.

1   The student makes so many errors in performing the skill or process important to the topic that he or she cannot actually perform the skill or process.

0   No judgment can be made.

Thinking and Reasoning Skills

Comparing and Contrasting

4   The student includes all important characteristics on which the items should be compared or contrasted.

3   The student includes the most important but not all characteristics on which the items should be compared or contrasted.

2   The student excludes some critical elements on which the items should be compared or contrasted.

1   The student uses trivial elements to compare or contrast the items.

0   No judgment can be made.

Analyzing Relationships

4   The student identifies the main (superordinate) pattern running through the information along with all minor (subordinate) patterns.

3   The student identifies the main (superordinate) pattern running through the information.

2   The student addresses some of the features of the main (superordinate) pattern running through the information but excludes some critical aspects.

1   The student does not address the main (superordinate) pattern running through the information.

0   No judgment can be made.

Classifying

4   The student organizes the items into meaningful categories and describes the defining characteristics of each category.

3   The student organizes the items into meaningful categories but does not thoroughly describe the defining characteristics of the categories.

2   The student organizes the items into categories that are not very meaningful but address some of the important characteristics of the items.

1   The student organizes the items into categories that are illogical or trivial.

0   No judgment can be made.

Argumentation

4   The student provides a well-articulated and detailed argument containing no errors in logic.

3   The student provides a well-articulated but not detailed argument containing no errors in logic.

2   The student presents an argument that makes a point but is not well articulated or contains some significant errors in logic.

1   The student's argument makes no clear point or has so many errors in logic that it is invalid.

0   No judgment can be made.

Induction

4   The student constructs a valid generalization and clearly articulates the logic of this generalization based on the specifics that have been identified.

3   The student constructs a valid generalization but does not clearly articulate the logic underlying that generalization.

2   The student constructs a generalization that has some relationship to the specifics that have been identified; however, the specifics do not totally support the generalization.

1   The student does not construct a generalization or constructs one that is not at all supported by the specifics.

0   No judgment can be made.

Deduction

4   The student generates a valid prediction or conclusion and accurately articulates the relationship between the prediction or conclusion and the principle or premise that was used.

3   The student generates a valid prediction or conclusion but does not completely articulate the relationship between the prediction or conclusion and the principle or premise that was used.

2   The student generates a prediction or conclusion that is only partially supported by the premise or rule that was used.

1   The student does not generate a prediction or conclusion or generates one that is not at all supported by the premise or rule that was used.

0   No judgment can be made.

Experimental Inquiry

4   The student designs and conducts an experiment that adequately tests a well-articulated hypothesis. When the experiment is completed, the student fully and accurately explains the results in light of the hypothesis.

3   The student designs and conducts an experiment that adequately tests a well-articulated hypothesis but does not completely explain the results in light of the hypothesis.

2   The student designs and conducts an experiment that is related to but does not adequately test the hypothesis.

1   The student does not design and conduct an experiment or designs one that has no relationship to the hypothesis.

0   No judgment can be made.

Investigation

4   The student thoroughly and accurately identifies what is known about the subject of the investigation and presents a well-articulated solution to the confusions or contradictions associated with the situation.

3   The student thoroughly and accurately identifies what is known about the subject of the investigation but does not fully address the confusions or contradictions associated with the situation.

2   The student presents a partial description of what is known about the subject of the investigation.

1   The student's description of what is known about the subject of the investigation is severely flawed.

0   No judgment can be made.

Problem Solving

4   The student selects the solution that is the most effective for overcoming the obstacle or constraint and accurately explains why it is the most effective of the possible solutions.

3   The student selects the solution that is the most effective for overcoming the obstacle or constraint but does not completely explain why it is the most effective of the possible solutions.

2   The student selects a solution that overcomes the obstacle or constraint but is not the most effective solution given the options.

1   The student selects a solution that does not overcome the obstacle or constraint.

0   No judgment can be made.

Decision Making

4   The student uses relevant criteria to select the most appropriate option. The student explains why the option selected is the most appropriate.

3   The student uses relevant criteria to select the most appropriate option but does not completely explain why the option selected is the most appropriate.

2   The student uses criteria that are related to the situation but not the most relevant, or the student selects an option that is not the most appropriate given the criteria.

1   The student uses criteria that are unrelated to the situation.

0   No judgment can be made.

Communication Skills

Communicates Effectively in Written Form

4   The student uses all necessary conventions of writing without error. Additionally, includes some conventions that are not essential to the communication but add to the overall quality of the communication.

3   The student uses all necessary conventions of writing without error.

2   The student does not use some required conventions of writing or demonstrates errors in the use of some conventions. The communication demonstrates an attempt at using the necessary conventions of writing but has significant errors or omissions.

1   The communication demonstrates little or no attention to the use of necessary conventions of writing.

0   No judgment can be made.

Communicates Effectively in Oral Form

4   The student uses all necessary conventions of speaking without error. Additionally, includes some conventions that are not essential to the communication but add to the overall quality of the communication.

3   The student uses all necessary conventions of speaking without error.

2   The student does not use some required conventions of speaking or demonstrates errors in the use of some conventions. The communication demonstrates an attempt at using the necessary conventions of speaking but has significant errors or omissions.

1   The communication demonstrates little or no attention to the use of the necessary conventions of speaking.

0   No judgment can be made.

Communicates Effectively in a Medium Other Than Writing or Speaking

4   The student uses all necessary conventions of the medium without error. Additionally, includes some conventions that are not essential to the communication but add to the overall quality of the communication.

3   The student uses all necessary conventions of the medium without error.

2   The student does not use some required conventions of the medium or demonstrates errors in the use of some conventions. The communication demonstrates an attempt at using the necessary conventions for the medium but has significant errors or omissions.

1   The communication demonstrates little or no attention to the use of the necessary conventions for the medium.

0   No judgment can be made.

Expresses Ideas Clearly

4   The student clearly and effectively communicates the main idea or theme and provides support that contains rich, vivid, and powerful detail.

3   The student clearly communicates the main idea or theme and provides suitable support and detail.

2   The student communicates important information but not a clear theme or overall structure.

1   The student communicates information as isolated pieces in a random fashion.

0   No judgment can be made.

Effectively Communicates with Diverse Audiences

4   The student presents information in a style and tone that effectively capitalizes on the audience's level of interest and level of knowledge or understanding.

3   The student presents information in a style and tone consistent with the audience's level of knowledge or understanding.

2   The student presents information in a style and tone inappropriate for the audience's level of interest or the audience's level of knowledge.

1   The student presents information in a style and tone inappropriate for both the audience's level of interest and level of knowledge.

0   No judgment can be made.

Effectively Communicates for a Variety of Purposes

4   The student clearly communicates a purpose in a highly creative and insightful manner.

3   The student uses effective techniques to communicate a clear purpose.

2   The student demonstrates an attempt to communicate for a specific purpose but makes significant errors or omissions.

1   The student demonstrates no central purpose in the communication or makes no attempt to articulate a purpose.

0   No judgment can be made.

Nonachievement Factors

EFFORT

Participation

4　The student participates in classroom activities and discussions without being asked.

3　The student participates in classroom activities and discussions when asked.

2　The student participates in classroom activities and discussions only when required to do so or when the request involves some form of explicit or implied threat.

1　The student refuses to engage in classroom activities and discussions.

0　No judgment can be made.

Assignments

4　The student is punctual or early turning in assignments and goes beyond the stated requirements relative to neatness and adherence to conventions.

3　The student is punctual in turning in assignments and meets the stated requirements relative to neatness and adherence to conventions.

2　The student is not punctual in turning in assignments or does not meet the stated requirements relative to neatness and adherence to conventions.

1　The student is not punctual in turning in assignments and does not meet the stated requirements relative to neatness and adherence to conventions.

0　No judgment can be made.

BEHAVIOR

Working in Groups

4　The student works toward the attainment of group goals without being asked.

3　The student works toward the attainment of group goals when asked or cued.

2　The student works toward the attainment of group goals only when required to do so or when the request involves strong urging or even some explicit or implicit threat.

1　The student refuses to work toward the attainment of group goals.

0　No judgment can be made.

Following Rules

4　The student follows classroom rules and procedures without being reminded or cued.

3   The student follows classroom rules and procedures when reminded or cued.

2   The student follows classroom rules and procedures only when required to do so or when the request involves strong urging or even some explicit or implicit threat.

1   The student refuses to follow classroom rules and procedures.

0   No judgment can be made.

ATTENDANCE

Absenteeism

4   The student is present.

3   The student is absent but provides a valid explanation or excuse.

2   The student is absent but provides a questionable explanation or excuse.

1   The student is absent without explanation or excuse.

0   No judgment can be made.

Tardiness

4   The student is on time.

3   The student is tardy but provides a valid excuse.

2   The student is tardy and provides a questionable excuse.

1   The student is tardy without explanation or excuse.

0   No judgment can be made.

The power law of learning, introduced in Chapter 5, can be traced to the findings of Newell and Rosenbloom (1981) that almost all learning can be described in terms of a power function. The term *power function* refers to any function that has the following form:

$$y = mx^b$$

Where:
- y is the score that is being predicted or computed
- x is the score on which the prediction is based
- m is a weight that is multiplied by the x score
- b is a power to which the x score is raised

In terms of learning, x in the formula above stands for the number of practices an individual has had; y stands for the individual's performance on the skill being learned. To illustrate, consider the power law formula below:

$$y = 1.40x^{-.24}$$

Researcher John Anderson (1995) explains that this power formula describes a particular type of learning situation—specifically, how much time in seconds (the y score) it takes to recognize verbatim information that has been presented to someone after the various amounts of exposure to that information (the x score). Notice that in this formula the weight (m) has been computed to be 1.40 and the power (b) has been computed to be –.24. Using these quantities, we can accurately predict how long in seconds it will take someone to accurately recognize verbatim information. For example, if we assume that someone has been exposed to verbatim information 20 times, we substitute the quantity 20 for the x score. Raising this x score of 20 to the power of –.24 and then multiplying by 1.40 yields a y score of about .68. After 20 exposures to verbatim information, it takes about .68 seconds to accurately recognize the information.

The key to using the power law is to compute the weight, m, and the power, b, in the general formula $y = mx^b$. Many mathematical processes can be used. The easiest to use is to

Start with the formula:

$$y = mx + b$$

where   y = the predicted score

x = the number of the assessment in terms of when it occurred during the grading period. For example, if the first assessment given during a grading period was a quiz, the second assessment was a homework assignment, and the third assessment was a performance task, then the x score for the quiz would be 1, the x score for the homework assignment would be 2, and the x score for the performance task would be 3.

m = a weight that is applied to each x score

b = a constant that is added to the product of m times x

Use the following steps:

1. Order the data so that each score has a corresponding assessment number.
2. Transform each assessment number and each assessment score to its natural log form. This will make the formula y = mx + b a rough approximation of the formula $y = mx^b$.
3. Compute m using the formula:

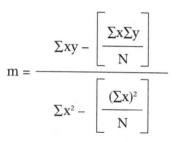

$$m = \frac{\Sigma xy - \left[\dfrac{\Sigma x \Sigma y}{N}\right]}{\Sigma x^2 - \left[\dfrac{(\Sigma x)^2}{N}\right]}$$

where N = number of assessments

4. Compute b using the formula:

$$b = \frac{\Sigma y - m(\Sigma x)}{N}$$

5. Identify the last assessment number in the set. For example, if 8 assessments were administered on a given topic, the last assessment number would be 8.
6. Enter the natural log of the last assessment number in the formula as the x variable.
7. Compute the right-hand portion of the formula (mx + b). This will provide the predicted score for the last assessment in logarithmic form.
8. Transform the quantity compiled in step #7 back to its original form. This is the predicted score for the last assessment in its original scale form.

References

Adelman, C. (1983). *Devaluation, diffusion, and the college connection: A study of high school transcripts 1964–1998*. Washington, DC: U.S. Department of Education. (ERIC Document Reproduction Service No. ED 228 244)

Airasian, P. W. (1994). *Classroom assessment* (2nd ed.). New York: McGraw-Hill.

American Association for the Advancement of Science. (1993). *Benchmarks for Science Literacy*. New York: Oxford University Press.

American Association for the Advancement of Science. (1989). *Science for all Americans: A Project 2061 report on literacy goals in science, mathematics, and technology*. Washington, DC: Author.

American Federation of Teachers. (1985, September). Critical thinking: It's a basic. *American Teacher*, 21.

American Federation of Teachers. (1998). *Making standards matter*. Washington, DC: Author.

Anderson, J. R. (1995). *Learning and memory: An integrated approach*. New York: John Wiley & Sons.

Atwell, N. C. (1987). *In the middle*. Portsmouth, NH: Heinemann.

Austin, S., & McCann, R. (1992, March). *Here's another arbitrary grade for your collection: A statewide study of grading policies*. Paper presented at the Annual Meeting of the American Educational Research Association, San Francisco, CA. (ERIC Document Reproduction Service No. 343 944)

Baker, J. R. (1974). *Race*. New York: Oxford University Press.

Baker, B. O., Hardwyck, C.D., & Petrinovich, L. F. (1966). Weak measurement vs. strong statistics: An empirical critique of S. S. Stevens' proscriptions on statistics. *Educational and Psychological Measurement, 26*, 291–309.

Baker, E. L., Aschbacher, P. R., Niemi, D., & Sato, E. (1992). *CRESST performance assessment models: Assessing content area explanations*. Los Angeles, CA: National Center for Research on Evaluation, Standards, and Student Testing (CRESST), University of California.

Berliner, D. C. (1984). The half-full glass: A review of research in teaching. In P. L. Hosford (Ed.), *Using what we know about teaching* (pp. 51–77). Alexandria, VA: Association for Supervision and Curriculum Development.

Beyer, B. K. (1988). *Developing a thinking skills program*. Boston: Allyn & Bacon.

Bock, R. D. (1997). A brief history of item response theory. *Educational Measurement: Issue and Practice, 16*(4), 21–33.

Boud, D., & Falchikov, N. (1989). Quantitative studies of student self-assessment in higher education: A critical analysis of findings. *Higher Education, 18*, 529–549.

Borko, H., Flory, M., & Cumbo, K. (1993, October). *Teachers' ideas and practices about assessment and instruction: A case study of the effects of alternative assessment in instruction, student learning, and accountability practice* (CSE Tech. Rep. No. 366). Los Angeles, CA: National Center for Research on Evaluation, Standards, and Student Testing (CRESST), University of California.

Bracey, G. (1994). Grade inflation. *Phi Delta Kappan, 4,* 328–329.

Brookhart, S. M. (1993). Teacher's grading practices: Meaning and values. *Journal of Educational Measurement, 30*(2), 123–142.

Brookhart, S. M. (1994). Teachers' grading: Practices and theory. *Applied Measurement in Education, 7*(4), 279–301.

Burke, C. J. (1953). Additive scales and statistics. *Psychological Review, 60,* 73–75.

Burt, C. (1957). The distribution of intelligence. *British Journal of Psychology, 48,* 161–175.

Calfee, R. C. (1994). *Implications for cognitive psychology for authentic assessment and instruction.* (Tech. Rep. No. 69). Berkeley, CA: National Center for the Study of Writing, University of California.

Calfee, R. C., & Hiebert, E. H. (1991). Classroom assessment of reading. In R. Barr, M. Kamil, P. Mosenthal, & P. D. Pearson (Eds.), *Handbook of research on reading* (2nd ed., pp. 281–309). New York: Longman.

Calkins, L. M. (1986). *The art of teaching writing.* Portsmouth, NH: Heinemann.

Cameron, J., & Pierce, W. D. (1994). Reinforcement, reward, and intrinsic motivation. *Review of Educational Research, 64*(3), 363–423.

Carnevale, A. P., Gainer, L. J., & Meltzer, A. S. (1990). *Workplace basics: The essential skills employers want.* San Francisco: Jossey-Bass.

Cazden, C. B. (1986). Classroom discourse. In M. C. Wittrock (Ed.), *Handbook of research on teaching* (3rd ed., pp. 432–463). New York: Macmillan.

Center for Civic Education. (1994). *National standards for civics and government.* Calabasas, CA: Author.

Clark, H. H., & Clark, E. V. (1977). *Psychology & language.* San Diego, CA: Harcourt Brace Jovanovich.

College Board, The (1983). *Academic preparation for college: What students need to know and be able to do.* New York: College Entrance Examination Board.

College Board, The (1997, August 26). *News from The College Board.* New York: Author.

College Board, The (1998). *High school grading policies.* (Research notes: RN-04). Princeton, NJ: Author.

Commission on the Humanities. (1980). *The humanities in American life.* Berkeley, CA: University of California Press.

Consortium of National Arts Education Associations. (1994). *National standards for arts education: What every young American should know and be able to do in the arts.* Reston, VA: Music Educators National Conference.

Countryman, L. L., & Schroeder, M. (1996, April). When students lead parent-teacher conferences. *Educational Leadership, 53,* 64–68.

Crafton, L. K. (1996). *Standards in practice: Grades K–2.* Urbana, IL: National Council of Teachers of English.

Cronbach, L. J., Bradburn, N. M., & Horvitz, D. G. (1994). *Sampling and statistical procedures used in the California Learning Assessment System.* Palo Alto, CA: The Select Committee.

Cross, C. T. (1997). Hard questions, "standard answers." *Basic Education, 42*(3), 1–3.

Cross, L. H., & Frary, R. B. (1999). Hodgepodge grading: Endorsed by students and teachers alike. *Applied Measurement in Education, 12*(1), 53–72.

Darling-Hammond, L., Ancess, J., & Falk, B. (1995). *Authentic assessment in action.* New York: Columbia University Press.

Davis, F. B. (1964). Measurement of change. In F. B. Davis (Ed.), *Educational measurements and their interpretations* (pp. 46–78). Belmont, CA: Woodsworth.

de Bono, E. (1985). The CoRT thinking program. In J. W. Segal, S. F. Chipman, & R. Glaser (Eds.), *Thinking and learning skills: Vol. 1. Relating instruction to research* (pp. 363–388). Hillsdale, NJ: Lawrence Erlbaum.

Dossey, J. A., Mullis, I. V. S., & Jones, C. O. (1993). *Can students do mathematical problem solving?* (pp. 116–117). Washington, DC: U.S. Department of Education, Office of Educational Research and Improvement.

Doyle, W. (1992). Curriculum and pedagogy. In P. W. Jackson (Ed.), *Handbook of research in curriculum* (pp. 465–485). New York: Macmillan.

Durm, M. W. (1993). An A is not an A is not an A: A history of grading. *The Educational Forum, 57*(Spring), 294–297.

Durst, R. K., & Newell, G. E. (1989). The uses of function: James Britton's category system and research on writing. *Review of Educational Research, 59*(4), 375–394.

Ebel, R. L. (1970). The case for true-false test items. *School Review, 78,* 373–389.

Educational Testing Service. (1987). *Learning by doing: A manual for teaching and assessing higher order thinking in science and mathematics.* Princeton, NJ: Author.

Education Week on the Web. (1998). Executive summary: The urban challenge. In *Quality counts 98* [Online]. Available: http://www.edweek.com/sreports/qc98/intros/in-n.htm.

Esty, W. W., & Teppo, A. R. (1992). Grade assignment based on progressive improvement. *The Mathematics Teacher, 85*(8), 616–618.

Falchikov, N., & Boud, D. (1989). Student self-assessment in higher education: A meta-analysis. *Review of Educational Research, 59,* 395–430.

Falk, B., & Darling-Hammond, L. (1993, March). *The primary language record at P. S. 261: How assessment transforms teaching and learning.* New York: National Center for Restructuring Education, Schools, and Teaching.

Farkas, S., Friedman, W., Boese, J., & Shaw, G. (1994). *First things first: What Americans expect from public schools.* New York: Public Agenda.

Finn, Jr., C. E., Petrilli, M. J., & Vanourek, G. (1998, November 11). The state of state standards: Four reasons why most "don't cut the mustard." *Education Week, 18,* pp. 39, 56.

Frary, R. B., Cross, L. H., & Weber, L. J. (1993). Testing and grading practices and opinions of secondary teachers of academic subjects: Implications for instruction in measurement. *Educational Measurement: Issues and Practice, 12*(3), 23–30.

Fuchs, L. S., & Fuchs, D. (1986). Effects of systematic formative evaluation: A meta-analysis. *Exceptional Children, 53*(3), 199–206.

Futrell, M. H. (1987, December 9). A message long overdue. *Education Week, 7*(14), 9.

Gandal, M. (1995). *Making standards matter: A fifty-state progress report on efforts to raise academic standards.* Washington, DC: American Federation of Teachers.

Gandal, M. (1996). *Making standards matter, 1996: An annual fifty-state report on efforts to raise academic standards.* Washington, DC: American Federation of Teachers.

Gandal, M. (1997). *Making standards matter, 1997: An annual fifty-state report on efforts to raise academic standards.* Washington, DC: American Federation of Teachers.

Geography Education Standards Project. (1994). *Geography for life: National geography standards.* Washington, DC: National Geographic Research and Exploration.

Glaser, R. (1984). Education and thinking: The role of knowledge. *American Psychologist, 39,* 93–104.

Glickman, C. (1993). *Reviewing America's schools.* San Francisco: Jossey-Bass.

Goodman, Y. M. (1978). Kid watching: An alternative to testing. *National Elementary School Principal, 57,* 41–45.

Gulliksen, H. (1950). *Theory of mental tests.* New York: John Wiley & Sons.

Guskey, T. R. (Ed.). (1996a). *Communicating student learning* (1996 ASCD Yearbook). Alexandria, VA: Association for Supervision and Curriculum Development.

Guskey, T. R. (1996b). Reporting on student learning: Lessons from the past—Prescriptions for the future. In T. R. Guskey (Ed.),

Communicating student learning (1996 ASCD Yearbook, pp. 13–24). Alexandria, VA: Association for Supervision and Curriculum Development.

Haladyna, T. M. (1992). The effectiveness of several multiple-choice formats. *Applied Measurement in Education, 5,* 73–88.

Haladyna, T. M. (1994). *Developing and validating multiple-choice test items.* Hillsdale, NJ: Erlbaum.

Haladyna, T. M. (1997). *Writing test items to evaluate higher order thinking.* Boston, MA: Allyn & Bacon.

Hansen, J. (1987). *When writers read.* Portsmouth, NH: Heinemann.

Hansen, J. (1994). Literacy portfolios: Windows on potential. In S. W. Valencia, E. H. Hiebert, & P. P. Afflerrbach (Eds.), *Authentic reading assessment: Practices and possibilities* (pp. 26–44). Newark, DE: International Reading Association.

Harrison, G. A., Weiner, J. S., Tanner, J. M., & Barnicot, N. A. (1964). *Human biology: An introduction to human evolution, variation, and growth.* London: Oxford University Press.

Hart, D. C. (1994). *Authentic assessment: A handbook for educators.* Menlo Park, CA: Addison-Wesley.

Hattie, J. A. (1992). Measuring the effects of schooling. *Australian Journal of Education, 36*(1), 5–13.

Hawkins, D. (1973). I, thou, it: The triangular relationship. In C. Silberman (Ed.), *The open classroom reader* (pp. 25–40). New York: Random House.

Heurnstein, R. J., & Murray, C. (1994). *The bell curve: Intelligence and class structure in American life.* New York: The Free Press.

Hirsch, E. D., Jr. (1987). *Cultural literacy: What every American needs to know.* Boston: Houghton Mifflin.

Hirsch, E. D., Jr. (1996). *The schools we need: Why we don't have them.* New York: Doubleday.

Hubbard, J. P. (1978). *Measuring medical education: The tests and the experience of the National Board of Medical Examiners* (2nd ed.). Philadelphia: Lea & Febiger.

Jensen, A. R. (1980). *Bias in mental testing.* New York: The Free Press.

Joint Committee on National Health Education Standards. (1995). *National health education standards: Achieving health literacy.* Reston, VA: Association for the Advancement of Health Education.

Keith, T. Z. (1982). Time spent on homework and high school grades: A large-sample path analysis. *Journal of Educational Psychology, 2,* 248–253.

Kendall, J. S., & Marzano, R. J. (1997). *Content knowledge: A compendium of standards and benchmarks for K–12 education* (2nd ed.). Alexandria, VA: Association for Supervision and Curriculum Development.

Kentucky Institute for Educational Research, The. (1995, January). *An independent evaluation of the Kentucky Instructional Results Information System (KIRIS): Executive summary.* Frankfort, KY: Author.

Khattri, N., Kane, M. B., & Reeve, A. L. (1995, November). How performance assessments affect teaching and learning. *Educational Leadership, 53,* 80–83.

Kleinsasser, A. (1991, September). *Rethinking assessment: Who's the expert?* Paper presented at the Casper Outcomes Conference: Casper, WY.

Knight, P. (1992, May). How I use portfolios in mathematics. *Educational Leadership, 49,* 71–72.

Kohn, A. (1993). *Punished by rewards: The trouble with gold stars, incentive plans, A's, praise and other bribes.* Boston: Houghton Mifflin.

Kohn, A. (1996). *Beyond discipline: From compliance to community.* Alexandria, VA: Association for Supervision and Curriculum Development.

Kohn, A. (1999). From grading to degrading. *High School Magazine, 6*(5), 38–48.

Leiter, J., & Brown, J. S. (1983). *Sources of elementary school grading* (Technical report). Raleigh, NC: North Carolina State University. (ERIC Document Reproduction Service No. 236-135)

Linn, R. L., & Gronlund, N. E. (1995). *Measurement and assessment in teaching* (7th ed.). Englewood Cliffs, NJ: Prentice-Hall.

Livingston, S. A. (1982). *Passing scores: A manual for setting standards of performance on educational and occupational tests*. Princeton, NJ: Educational Testing Service.

Lord, F. M., & Novick, M. R. (1968). *Statistical theories of mental test scores*. Reading, MA: Addison & Wesley.

Magnussen, D. (1966). *Test theory*. Reading, MA: Addison & Wesley.

Marzano, R. J. (1992a). *A different kind of classroom: Teaching with dimensions of learning*. Alexandria, VA: Association for Supervision and Curriculum Development.

Marzano, R. J. (1992b). *Dimensions of learning: A new paradigm for curriculum, instruction, and assessment*. Unpublished paper, Mid-continent Regional Educational Laboratory, Aurora, Colorado.

Marzano, R. J. (1995a). *Independent grades provided by team-teachers*. Unpublished data, Mid-continent Regional Educational Laboratory, Aurora, Colorado.

Marzano, R. J. (1995b). *Teacher report of use of variables when constructing grades*. Unpublished data, Mid-continent Regional Educational Laboratory, Aurora, Colorado.

Marzano, R. J. (1998a). *Findings from multiple studies of independent grades assigned by team-teachers*. Unpublished data, Mid-continent Regional Educational Laboratory, Aurora, Colorado.

Marzano, R. J. (1998b). What are the general skills of thinking and reasoning and how do you teach them? *The Clearing House, 71*(5), 268–273.

Marzano, R. J. (1999). Building curriculum and assessment around standards. *The High School Magazine, 6*(5), 14–19.

Marzano, R. J. (2000). *Analyzing two assumptions underlying the scoring of classroom assessments* (Technical report). Aurora, CO: Mid-continent Research for Education and Learning.

Marzano. R. J., & Kendall, J. S. (1996). *A comprehensive guide to designing standards-based districts, schools, and classrooms*. Alexandria, VA: Association for Supervision and Curriculum Development/Aurora, CO: Mid-continent Regional Educational Laboratory.

Marzano, R. J., Kendall, J. S., & Cicchinelli, L. F. (1998). *What Americans believe students should know: A survey of U. S. adults*. Aurora, CO: Mid-continent Regional Educational Laboratory.

Marzano, R. J., Kendall, J. S., & Gaddy, B. B. (1999). *Essential knowledge: The debate over what American students should know*. Aurora, CO: Mid-continent Regional Educational Laboratory.

Marzano, R. J., Mayeski, F., & Dean, C. (1999). *Standards in the classroom*. Aurora, CO: Mid-continent Regional Educational Laboratory.

Marzano, R. J., Pickering, D. J., & McTighe, J. (1993). *Assessing student outcomes: Performance assessment using the dimensions of learning model*. Alexandria, VA: Association for Supervision and Curriculum Development.

McMillan, J. (in press). *Basic assessment concepts for teachers*. Thousand Oaks, CA: Corwin Press.

McMillan, J. H. (1997). *Classroom assessment: Principles and practices for effective instruction*. Needham Heights, MD: Allyn & Bacon.

Meyer, C. A. (1992, May). What's the difference between authentic and performance assessment? *Educational Leadership, 49*, 39–40.

National Association for Sport and Physical Education. (1995). *Moving into the future, national standards for physical education: A guide to content and assessment*. St. Louis, MO: Mosby.

National Center for History in the Schools. (1996). *National standards for history: Basic edition*. Los Angeles: University of California, Author.

National Council for the Social Studies. (1994). *Expectations of excellence: Curriculum standards for social studies*. Washington, DC: Author.

National Council of Teachers of Mathematics. (1989). *Curriculum and evaluation standards for school mathematics.* Reston, VA: Author.

National Education Goals Panel (1991). *The national education goals report: Building a nation of learners.* Washington, DC: Author.

National Research Council. (1996). *National science education standards.* Washington, DC: National Academy Press.

National Science Board Commission on Precollege Education in Mathematics, Science and Technology. (1983). *Educating Americans for the 21st century.* Washington, DC: Author.

National Standards in Foreign Language Education Project. (1996). *Standards for foreign language learning: Preparing for the 21st century.* Lawrence, KS: Author.

Nava, F. J. G., & Loyd, B. H. (1992, April). *An investigation of achievement and non-achievement criteria in elementary and secondary school grading.* Paper presented at the Annual Meeting of the American Educational Research Association, San Francisco, CA. (ERIC Document Reproduction Service No. ED 346 145)

Newell, A., & Rosenbloom, P. S. (1981). Mechanisms of skill acquisition and the law of practice. In J. R. Anderson (Ed.), *Cognitive skills and their acquisition.* Hillsdale, NJ: Erlbaum.

Newmann, F. M., Secado, W. G., & Wehlage, G. G. (1995). *A guide to authentic instruction and assessment: Vision, standards and scoring.* Madison, WI: Wisconsin Center for Educational Research, University of Wisconsin.

O'Connor, K. (1995). Guidelines for grading that support learning and success. *NASSP Bulletin, 79*(571), 91–101.

O'Donnell, A., & Woolfolk, A. E. (1991). *Elementary and secondary teachers' beliefs about testing and grading.* Paper presented at the annual meeting of the American Psychological Association, San Francisco, CA.

Olson, L. (1995, June 14). Cards on the table. *Education Week,* 23–28.

Ornstein, A. C. (1994). Grading practices and policies: An overview and some suggestions. *NASSP Bulletin, 78*(561), 55–64.

Pilcher, J. K. (1994). The value-driven meaning of grades. *Educational Assessment, 1*(1), 69–88.

Quellmalz, E. S. (1987). Developing reasoning skills. In J. B. Baron & R. J. Sternberg (Eds.), *Teaching thinking skills: Theory and practice.* New York: W. H. Freeman.

Resnick, L. B. (1987). *Education and learning to think.* Washington, DC: National Academy Press.

Resnick, L. B., & Resnick, D. P. (1992). Assessing the thinking curriculum: New tools for educational reform. In B. R. Gifford & M. C. O'Connor (Eds.), *Changing assessments: Alternative views of aptitude, achievement and instruction* (pp. 37–76). Boston: Kluwer Academic Press.

Robinson, G. E., & Craver, J. M. (1989). *Assessing and grading student achievement.* Arlington, VA: Educational Research Service.

Secretary's Commission on Achieving Necessary Skills, The (1991). *What work requires of schools: A SCANS Report for America 2000.* Washington, DC: U.S. Department of Labor.

Senders, V. L. (1953). A comment on Burke's additive scales and statistics. *Psychological Review, 60,* 423–424.

Shavelson, R. J., & Baxter, G. P. (1992, May). What we've learned about assessing hands-on science. *Educational Leadership, 49,* 20–25.

Shavelson, R. J., & Webb, N. M. (1991). *Generalizability theory: A primer.* Newbury Park, CA: Sage Publishing.

Shavelson, R. J., Gao, X., & Baxter, G. R. (1993). *Sampling variability of performance assessments* (Report No. 361). Santa Barbara, CA: University of California, National Center for Research in Evaluation, Standards and Student Testing.

Shavelson, R. J., Webb, N. M., & Rowley, G. (1989). Generalizability theory. *American Psychologist, 44*(6), 922–932.

Shepard, L.A. (1991). Psychometricians' beliefs about learning. *Educational Researcher, 20*(7), 2–16.

Sierra-Perry, M. (1996). *Standards in practice: Grades 3–5.* Urbana, IL: National Council of Teachers of English.

Simon, S. B., & Bellanca, J. A. (Eds.) (1976). *Re-grading the grading myths: Primer of alternatives to grades and marks.* Alexandria, VA: Association for Supervision and Curriculum Development.

Smagorinski, P. (1996). *Standards in practice: Grades 9–12.* Urbana, IL: National Council of Teachers of English.

Smith, M. L., Noble, A. J., Cabay, M., Heinecke, W., Junker, M. S., & Saffron, Y. (1994, July). *What happens when the test mandate changes? Results of a multiple case study* (Report No. 380). Los Angeles, CA: National Center for Research on Evaluation, Standards, and Student Testing (CRESST), University of California.

Sperling, D. (1996). Collaborative assessment: Making high standards a reality for all students. In R. E. Blum & J. A. Arter (Eds.), *A handbook for student performance assessment in an era of restructuring* (pp. iv–11). Alexandria, VA: Association for Supervision and Curriculum Development.

State of Florida, Department of State (1996). *Science: Pre K–12 sunshine state standards and instructional practices.* Tallahassee, FL: Author.

Staton, J. (1980). Writing and counseling: Using a dialogue journal. *Language Arts, 57,* 514–518.

Stevens, S. S. (1946). On the theory of scales of measurement. *Science, 103,* 677–680.

Stevenson, H. W., & Stigler, J. W. (1992). *The learning gap: Why our schools are failing and what we can learn from Japanese and Chinese education.* New York: Touchstone.

Stiggins, R. J. (1994). *Student-centered classroom assessment.* New York: Merrill.

Stiggins, R. J. (1997). *Student-centered classroom assessment* (2nd ed.). Columbus, OH: Merrill.

Stiggins, R. J., & Conklin, N. F. (1992). *In Teachers' hands: Investigating the practice of classroom assessment.* Albany, NY: SUNY Press.

Stiggins, R. J., Frisbie, D. A., & Griswold, P. A. (1989). Inside high school grading practices: Building a research agenda. *Educational Measurement: Issues and Practices, 8*(2), 5–14.

Stodolsky, S. S. (1989). Is teaching really by the book? In P. W. Jackson & S. Haroutunian-Gordon (Eds.), *Eighty-ninth yearbook of the national society for the study of education, Part I* (pp. 159–184). Chicago: University of Chicago Press.

Szetela, W., & Nicol, C. (1992, May). Evaluating problem solving in mathematics. *Educational Leadership, 49,* 42–45.

Terwilliger, J. S. (1971). *Assigning grades to students.* Glenview, IL: Scott, Foresman & Co.

Terwilliger, J. S. (1989, Summer). Classroom standard setting and grading practices. *Educational Measurement: Issues and Practice,* 15–19.

Thaiss, C. (1986). *Language across the curriculum in the elementary grades.* Urbana, IL: ERIC Clearinghouse on Reading and Communication Skills and National Council of Teachers of English.

Topping, K. (1998). Peer assessment between students in college and universities. *Review of Educational Research, 68*(8), 249–276.

Turnbill, W. W. (1985). *Student change, program change: Why SAT scores kept falling* (College Board Report No. 85-2). New York: College Entrance Examination Board.

Tyack, T., & Tobin, W. (1994). The "grammar" of schooling: Why has it been so hard to change. *American Educational Research Journal, 31*(3), 453–479.

U.S. Department of Education, Office of Educational Research and Improvement (1994). *What do student grades mean? Differences across schools.* (Office of Research Report 94-3401). Washington, DC: Office of Educational Research and Improvement.

Valencia, S. (1987, April). *Novel formats for assessing prior knowledge and measures of read-*

ing comprehension. Paper presented at the Annual Meeting of the American Educational Research Association, Washington, DC.

Valencia, S. W., Stallman, A. C., Commeyras, M., Pearson, P. D., & Hartman, D. K. (1991). Four measures of topical knowledge: A study of construct validity. *Reading Research Quarterly, 26*(3), 204–233.

Wentzel, K. R. (1991). Classroom competence may require more than intellectual ability: Reply to Jussim (1991). *Journal of Educational Psychology, 83*(1), 156–158.

Wiggins, G. (1993a, November). Assessment, authenticity, context and validity. *Phi Delta Kappan,* 200–214.

Wiggins, G. P. (1993b). *Assessing student performances: Exploring the purpose and limits of testing.* San Francisco: Jossey-Bass.

Wiggins, G. (1994, November). Toward better report cards. *Educational Leadership, 52,* 28–37.

Wiggins, G. (1996). Honesty and fairness: Toward better grading and reporting. In T. R. Guskey (Ed.), *ASCD yearbook 1996: Communicating student learning* (pp. 141–177). Alexandria, VA: Association for Supervision and Curriculum Development.

Wiggins, G. (1998). *Educative assessment: Designing assessments to inform and improve student performance.* San Francisco, CA: Jossey-Bass.

Wilburn, K. T., & Felps, B. C. (1983). *Do pupil grading methods affect middle school students' achievement: A comparison of criterion-referenced versus norm-referenced evaluations.* Unpublished document. Jacksonville, FL: Wolfson H. S. (ERIC Document Reproduction Service No. ED 229 451)

Wilde, S. (Ed.). (1996). *Notes from a kid watcher: Selected writings of Yetta M. Goodman.* Portsmouth, NH: Heinemann.

Wilhelm, J. D. (1996). *Standards in practice: Grades 6–8.* Urbana, IL: National Council of Teachers of English.

Winograd, P., & Webb, K. S. (1994). Impact on curriculum and instruction. In T. R. Guskey (Ed.), *High stakes performance assessment: Perspectives on Kentucky's educational reform* (pp. 19–36). Thousand Oaks, CA: Corwin Press.

Wood, L. A. (1994). An unintended impact of one grading practice. *Urban Education, 29*(2), 188–201.

Wright, D., & Wise, M. J. (1988). Teacher judgment in student evaluation: A comparison of grading methods. *Journal of Educational Research, 82*(1), 10–14.

Wrinkle, W. L. (1947). *Improving marking and reporting practices in elementary and secondary schools.* New York: Holt, Rinehart and Winston.

Yoon, B., Burstein, L., & Gold, K. (n.d.). *Assessing the content validity of teachers' reports of content coverage and its relationship to student achievement* (CSE Rep. No. 328). Los Angeles, CA: National Center for Research on Evaluation, Standards, and Student Testing (CRESST), University of California.

Young, A., & Fulwiler, T. (Eds.). (1986). *Writing across the disciplines.* Portsmouth, NH: Heinemann.

Zeidner, M. (1992). Key facets of classroom grading: A comparison of teacher and student perspectives. *Contemporary Educational Psychology, 17*(3), 224–243.

Zlomek, R. L., & Svec, J. C. (1997). High school grades and achievement: Evidence of grade inflation. *NASSP Bulletin, 81*(587), 105–113.

Index

Note: References to figures are followed by *f.*

About the Author

Robert J. Marzano is a Senior Fellow at Mid-continent Research for Education and Learning (McREL) in Aurora, Colorado. He is responsible for translating research and theory into classroom practice. He headed a team of authors who developed *Dimensions of Learning* published by the Association for Supervision and Curriculum Development (ASCD), and is also the senior author of *Tactics for Thinking* (ASCD) and *Literacy Plus: An Integrated Approach to Teaching Reading, Writing, Vocabulary, and Reasoning* (Zaner-Bloser). His most recent efforts address standards as described in the two books *Essential Knowledge: The Debate Over What American Students Should Know* (Marzano, Kendall, & Gaddy, McREL, 1999) and *A Comprehensive Guide to Designing Standards-Based Districts, Schools, and Classrooms* (Marzano & Kendall, ASCD/McREL, 1996). He has also recently completed a book entitled *Designing a New Taxonomy of Educational Objectives* published by Corwin Press. He has developed programs and practices used in K–12 classrooms that translate current research and theory in cognition into instructional methods.

Marzano received his B.A. in English from Iona College in New York, an M.Ed. in Reading/Language Arts from Seattle University, Seattle, Washington, and a Ph.D. in Curriculum and Instruction from the University of Washington, Seattle. Prior to his work with McREL, Marzano was a tenured associate professor at the University of Colorado at Denver, and a high school English teacher and department chair.

An internationally known trainer and speaker, Marzano has authored 18 books and over 150 articles and chapters in books on such topics as reading and writing instruction, thinking skills, school effectiveness, restructuring, assessment, cognition, and standards implementation.

He may be contacted at McREL, 2550 S. Parker Rd., Suite 500, Aurora, CO 80014. Phone: 303-632-5534. Fax: 303-337-3005. E-mail: bmarzano@mcrel.org.

Related ASCD Resources: Grading

ASCD stock numbers are noted in parentheses.

Audiotapes

Alternative Ways to Document and Communicate Student Learning by Tom Guskey and David Johnson (#296211)

Assessment and Grading: What's the Relationship? (#496273)

Current Grading Practices that Decrease the Odds for Student Success by Robert Canady (#61293080)

Standards-Based Grading for the Classroom by Robert J. Marzano (#200157)

Print Products

Communicating Student Learning, edited by Thomas R. Guskey (#196000)

A Comprehensive Guide to Designing Standards-Based Districts, Schools, and Classrooms by Robert J. Marzano and John S. Kendall (#196215)

Content Knowledge: A Compendium of Standards and Benchmarks for K–12 Education (2nd ed.) by John S. Kendall and Robert J. Marzano (#598048)

Reporting What Students Are Learning [Special Issue]. *Educational Leadership* v. 52, n. 2 (#1-94212)

Professional Inquiry Kit

Promoting Learning Through Student Data, developed by Marian Leibowitz (#999004)

Videotape

Reporting Student Progress (#495249)

For additional resources, visit us on the World Wide Web (http://www.ascd.org), send an e-mail message to member@ascd.org, call the ASCD Service Center (1-800-933-ASCD or 703-578-9600, then press 2), send a fax to 703-575-5400, or write to Information Services, ASCD, 1703 N. Beauregard St., Alexandria, VA 22311-1714 USA.